Discovering
The Dales Way

Featuring People, Places and Histories

Keith Pauling

First published 2010

ISBN 978-1-4466-3705-0

By the same author

Thames Pathway

Map of the Dales Way

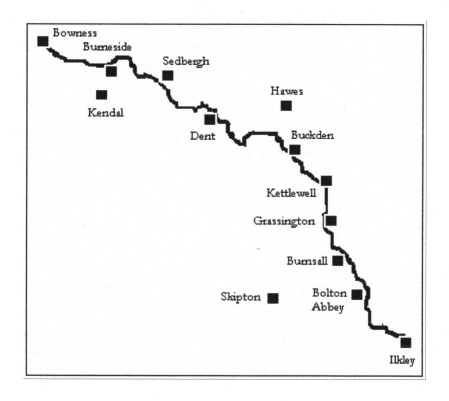

INTRODUCTION

The "Dales Way" passes through some of the most beautiful scenery in England.

The footpath is 84 miles in length and runs from Ilkley to Bowness-on-Windermere. Starting on the banks of the River Wharfe it follows the river upstream, climbs over the top of the watershed of the Pennines, and then winds steadily down the other side passing through the delightful undulating countryside of where we once used to call Westmorland, before finally arriving at the shore of England's largest expanse of inland water.

Along the way I will be exploring the places that I visit and delving into the histories of the people who have made their contributions to life in the area throughout the ages.

Join me on my journey and discover our rich heritage.

Cover Photographs

| Upper; | Ewe and Lamb, Upper Wharfedale |
| Lower; | Drystone Enclosures, Kettlewell |

DAY ONE

ILKLEY TO GRASSINGTON

16.3 MILES

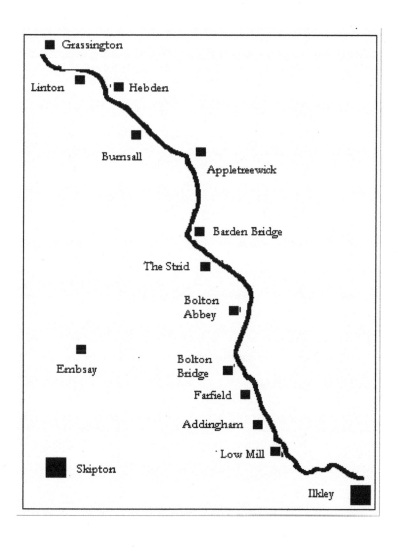

Ilkley

The one thing that most people know about Ilkley is that you really shouldn't go there without wearing your hat.

This is indelibly imprinted in our minds because those of us of a certain age vividly remember the many coach journeys of our childhood years when we were at school or members of the scouts and guides. One of the favourite ways in which to alleviate the boredom of the journey was for some of the more raucous pimply youths (who always seemed to be occupying the back seats) to strike up in shrill tones "Where 'ast tha' bin since I saw thee........." and half the bus would sing (and I use the word loosely) back in answer "On Ilkley Moor bah't hat". The remainder of the journey would then simply fly past, filled by the cautionary tale of the young Yorkshire lad who went a-courting Mary Jane being severely warned that this would only result in him catching his death of cold and being 'et up by worms. If he hadn't got the fatal message before the last verse the young Romeo was cautioned once again not to venture on to the moor without his hat on.

Mary Jane must have been a very popular girl to have been worth all of that trouble!

However it is not the romantic charms of a comely local lass that brings me to this picturesque town in West Yorkshire. I am here because Ilkley marks the southern end of the Dales Way which I am going to be following all the way to its northern finishing point at Bowness-on-Windermere.

This year (2009) sees the celebration of the 40th anniversary of this long-distance footpath, and there will be many others who will be making their footprints along the same route over the next few months.

I have chosen early May for my walk in the anticipation of enjoying some fine early spring weather. It is certainly a glorious sunny day today and although 10am is still relatively early for a Saturday morning there are plenty of other people who are also out and about enjoying the day.

Ilkley has a population of around 15,000 people and is approximately 18 miles northwest of the city of Leeds. The town sits on the south bank of the River Wharfe, one of Yorkshire's finest rivers. The beautifully scenic upper reaches of the Wharfe valley extend to the north, and the famous Ilkley Moor lies to the south. The locality has been continuously inhabited since around 1800BC and there is some evidence of stone tools dating back even further to the Mesolithic Period some 13,000 years ago.

The Romans settled here around 79AD and constructed a small fort that they named Olicana. Despite its diminutive size the fort played an important role in keeping the local rebellious Brigantes tribe under some degree of control.

All Saints Church occupies a site that has been used for Christian worship since 627AD. The current church was largely rebuilt during the Victorian era, but still proudly contains a small collection of medieval and Saxon artifacts from its earlier days.

No history of an old established settlement in England is ever complete unless it can claim a reference in the Domesday Book of 1086. Ilkley is no exception, and the register records the manor of Ilkley as being in the possession of William de Percy, the first Baron Percy.

Things seem to have been relatively quiet around here for quite some while after the arrival of the Normans, so we can fast-forward through medieval times to the 17th and 18th centuries when the area around Ilkley became celebrated for the efficacy of its waters. Ilkley became a noted spa town, and the largest establishment, Ben Rhydding Hydro, was opened in 1843-44 in the nearby village of Wheatley.

The town seems proud of having a connection with the distinguished biologist and pioneer of the theory of evolution, Charles Darwin. There is a small park in his name at the edge of the moor, complete with a memorial plaque. It is not that Charles Darwin actually carried out any of his research work at Ilkley, but the somewhat tenuous connection is that the great man was rather partial to the local waters and stayed for a while at Wells House. This appears to have been sufficient justification for the local residents to commemorate his name for their town park.

The spa hydros have all gone now, but in their hey-day they were very popular and made a significant contribution to the prosperity of the local economy.

There are two places in Ilkley that simply have to be visited before I set off. Firstly I must leave the diet books at home and indulge myself in Bettys Tea Room.

Bettys Café Tea Room

Let me deal with the apostrophe pedants first. There has never been an apostrophe in the title of the establishment, so whether there was just one Betty or a whole tribe of Bettys has to be left to our imagination. In all probability there was never a Betty at all. There are several different stories about why the business is called Bettys, but the one I like the most is that when the first tea-room was founded in Harrogate there was a meeting of all of the investors to decide upon the name. The participants could not agree on a suitable name and at some point during this impasse a small girl wandered into the meeting room. When she announced that her name was Betty somebody suggested why not simply call it Bettys Cafe Tea Room and that was that. The establishment has been known as Bettys ever since.

The founder of the enterprise was a Swiss confectioner by the name of Frederick Belmont. For some reason Frederick decided to leave his native Switzerland to set up in business on the south coast of England. When Belmont arrived in London he became so confused with the strange language and the hustle and bustle of the city that instead of catching a train to the south he boarded a train to Yorkshire instead. When he arrived in Yorkshire young Frederick was so taken with the scenery that he decided that he would open his business here instead. So it was that in 1919 the first Bettys Café Tea Room was opened in Harrogate.

Frederick Belmont had an eye for detail and was one of those people for whom only the highest standards were ever acceptable. He applied these strict standards to his fledgling business and the enterprise blossomed. There are now Bettys Tea Rooms in six Yorkshire towns, including the very smart premises in The Grove, Ilkley.

The elegant shop-front is adorned with stained-glass images of flowers and other motifs. Walk inside and it like going back in time to a bygone age of gentility. I pass through the shop and enter the tea-room at the rear. The main tea-room is surprisingly light and airy. This effect is created by two of the walls being mirrored, whilst the long wall at the back is made up of a full series of upright window panels with more stained glass motifs. The fourth wall features a woodland hunting scene created in marquetry. There are a surprising number of tables, each surrounded by a combination of padded bench-seats and wicker-work chairs. There is a collection of china teapots adorning the walls. Most important of all there are mouth-watering cakes and biscuits on display in abundance. Fully aware of how many calories I will be burning up over the next few days it obviously makes great sense to put some reserves in the tank.

Despite the number of tables and the fact that it was only mid-morning the place was already full. I had to wait a few minutes for a vacancy to occur and for one of the waitresses to clear the table before I was led to a place. All of the waiters and waitresses were dressed in smart white tops with black skirts or trousers and a black apron. A pleasant change from the standard cheap polo-shirt embroidered with the business's logo used by so many other establishments as a uniform.

Up until the waitress placed the menu in my hand my intention was to simply ask for a coffee and a slice of fruit cake, but a quick glance at the menu soon made it clear that this was not going to be as simple as I had first thought. For a start instead of the typical piece of A4 card with the standard selection of beverages and a few snacks I was holding in my hand a mouth-watering booklet of confectionery and a staggering choice of blended teas and coffees.

I only live a couple of miles downwind of the "Kenco Coffee" manufacturing plant so the aroma of ground coffee is often in the air. However there was nothing here as simple and straightforward as being able to obtain a cup of my "local brew". The coffee list was a veritable gourmet guide to the dark aromatic liquid. What on earth is "Bosque Lya Apple Grove" when it's at home? The guide helpfully informed me that this particular beverage was made from the finest beans that El Salvador could supply. Should I plump for this or take a chance on the "Ethiopian Mocha Limu? I notice that among the list of candidates competing for my attention is the marvelously alliterative simple name of "Java Jampit". I finally decide that on the name alone I must try it; and it was indeed excellent.

Tea drinkers would fare no better. How could anyone possibly choose between "Ntingwe Estate Kwazalu" and "Yu Luo White Tea"? One could spend weeks in here and not sample all of the exotic varieties which everywhere else refers to as simply tea or coffee.

It turned out that picking the drink was easy compared to the food. While I was sorely tempted by the "Yorkshire Fat Rascal" (which for some reason conjured up in my mind images of the fictional Detective Superintendent Dalziel morphed with a bun) I eventually decided that "Celebration Fruit Cake with Wensleydale Cheese" was the most fitting last meal before I set out on the walk. It was delicious.

Why in restaurants does the staff have to keep coming round to ask if everything is OK? It is one of my pet hates and I find myself mumbling "Yes, fine" and then a few moments later thinking of the smart response that I wished I had come up with a few seconds before. Not so this time. As soon as the young lady had uttered the words and before I fully realised what was happening my mouth sparkly replied "Cracking cheese eh Grommit?" The wry smile informed me that she had heard it before.

Ilkley Toy Museum

No visit to Ilkley would be complete without setting foot in the famous Toy Museum. Tucked away in a back-street almost opposite to the railway station the museum is a private collection of children's toys that stir the memories and take me back many years. So many toys that I remember from my own early days are on display. There are the soldiers and the Thunderbirds models which would regularly save the world from evil in my fertile childhood imagination. There are also Corgi cars and teddy bears and so much more to take me back in time. All of these nostalgic memories were mine for the entry fee of just £3.

I was fascinated by the working fairground. Brightly coloured carousels revolved and the helter-skelter stood proud among the painted fairground stalls.

There are dolls houses that were made with attention to immaculate detail. The main exhibit is "Stafford House", a model of a terraced house dating from 1830. To my mind, however, it is the model pet shop and butchers shop that are the best examples. Tiny model carcasses hang from the racking in the butchers, whilst even tinier model pets sit in their cages in the pet shop.

On the first floor there is a full wild-west scene with model cowboys and Indians, evoking memories of when I used to imitate the characters on "Wagon Train" and "The Virginian".

There are three prize exhibits that the museum is highly proud of. There is the oldest exhibit, an Etruscan doll dating back to around 350BC. A relatively more recent doll, but still an antique is known as "Miss Borwick" and is a Georgian lady from circa 1750 to 1760, complete with monogrammed sedan chair. Finally there is "Blanche", a 1910 white mohair Steiff teddy-bear that originally belonged to a Jewish-German girl. The bear, along with its owner, escaped to England at the start of the war and has since enjoyed appearing as a character in a book and also in a film.

All in all it was a wonderful trip back into nostalgia and well worth a visit if you are in the area. Be careful to check for opening times because they are generally limited to weekends only except at the height of summer.

Where Hast Tha Bin?

Before finally leaving Ilkley behind there is just time to find out a little more about the famous song. Some local people claim this to be the "National Anthem" of Yorkshire.

The first official publication of the song was in 1916, but allegedly it predates that time and it is reckoned to be more likely to have originated from the period between 1860 and 1880. According to local legend the song was composed by a visiting church choir from Halifax while they were enjoying a day trip to Ilkley Moor.

The tune is derived from a Methodist Hymn Tune known as "Cranbrook", written by Canterbury shoe-maker Thomas Clark in 1805. Originally the tune was used as a setting for the carol "While Shepherds Watched". You can try this for yourself in the manner of "I'm Sorry I Haven't a Clue" by singing one song to the tune of another. It fits together very well and now you know the reason why. Quite sensibly the tune is no longer used for hymns in this country because of the Ilkley version, but it is still in common use in the USA where it is used for the secular song "Grace! 'Tis a charming sound".

(As an aside, while researching this item, I stumbled upon a much more startling example of a Christmas Carol that can be sung to a completely different tune. You can sing "O Little Town of Bethlehem" to the tune of "House of the Rising Sun". Try it. It fits absolutely perfectly).

For anyone not familiar with "Ilkley Moor Baht 'At", each verse is made up by replacing lines 1, 3 and 4 with the next line in the list

Wheear 'ast tha bin sin' ah saw thee, ah saw thee?

On Ilkla Mooar baht 'at

Wheear 'ast t bin sin' ah saw thee, ah saw thee?

Wheear 'ast tha bin sin' ah saw thee?

On Ilkla Mooar baht 'at

On Ilkla Mooar baht 'at

On Ilkla Mooar baht 'at

2. Tha's been a courtin' Mary Jane

3. Tha's bahn to catch thy death o` cowd

4. Then us'll ha' to bury thee

5. Then t'worms'll come an` eyt thee up

6. Then t'ducks'll come an` eyt up t'worms

7. Then us'll go an` eyt up t'ducks

8. Then us'll all ha' etten thee

9. That's wheear we get us ooan back

The song chastises the young Romeo for wooing his young lady without the protection of appropriate headgear for the wild moorland. It continues by warning him that he would die of exposure and all the unfortunate consequences that would bring. In a way it was a sort of Victorian "Health and Safety" warning.

Ilkley Moor

Ilkley Moor itself is the highest part of the larger Rombald's Moor that rises to a height of 1319 feet (402m). The name "Rombald" is derived from the de Romilles family who held the nearby manor of Skipton in the thirteenth century.

As I see it today in the morning sunshine Ilkley Moor is a multicoloured background of purples and greys with bright green splashes of trees and even brighter clumps of bright yellow gorse. It looks an inviting place for a gentle saunter around the slopes without any need for protective headgear.

The terrain is mostly formed of millstone grit (a form of sandstone) outcrops interspersed with peat bogs. The most famous rock feature on the moor is commonly known as the "Cow and

Calf". This is an outcrop of millstone grit that forms the cow, with a nearby large boulder resembling the calf.

There is a further interesting aspect of Rombald's Moor, and that is that it possesses the second largest collection of ancient stone carvings in Europe. The area is liberally scattered with stones displaying many patterned carvings of cups, rings and grooves. Some of these patterns have been worn down by many centuries of exposure to the elements to be just feint scratches in the rock, but many others remain quite clearly distinguished. In some instances the patterns are quite complex. At Woodhouse Crag on the northerly edge of Ilkley Moor the famous "Swastika Stone" can be found. Other well noted examples include the Badger Stone and St Margaret's Stones. Finally there is a small stone circle known as the "Twelve Apostles".

The Start of the Trail

The official start to the Dales Way is situated at the "Old Bridge". This is an old packhorse bridge spanning the fast flowing waters of the River Wharfe. The bridge was built in the 1670's and provides an excellent photo opportunity with which to mark the starting point. A low weir of only a few inches generates a narrow line of white water immediately downstream of the twin arches. Freshly-leaved trees enable me to frame the stone bridge under an arch of green. The shutters click and the moment will stay forever.

The official starting point is marked with the obligatory notice board showing the route ahead along with a brief description of the terrain. Nearby is a stone slab with a small cairn bearing a plaque announcing "For those who walk the Dales Way". In six days time I will come across a similar slab on the hillside above Bowness-on-Windermere that marks the opposite end of the trail.

The first part of the walk follows a broad path and then passes a very fine looking tennis club. The courts are being put to good use this fine Saturday morning with a whole variety of different age groups exchanging shots with the steady "thwack" of racket on ball punching through the air. There are a few balls lying on my path, the results of several wayward shots. I lob them back over the perimeter fencing to their owners and receive appreciative smiles and shouts of thanks in return.

I soon emerge on to the riverbank and follow the well-worn path upstream towards Low Mill. The river sparkles as the sunlight reflects from its gentle ripples.

I will be walking alongside the River Wharfe for most of the next two days so it is worth looking at the geography of the river in more detail. The Wharfe has its source at Cam Fell where I will be crossing the Pennines in two days time. From the source down to Addingham, which is the first village that I will encounter on my journey, the valley is generally referred to as Upper Wharfedale. Below where I have rejoined the river it flows through Ilkley, Otley, Wetherby and Tadcaster before joining the River Ouse near Cawood. In total the river flows for some 60 miles (93Km) and drains a large area of Yorkshire. It is a beautiful river, but it is also deceptively dangerous. Many people have come to an untimely end by underestimating the power of its swift currents that can quickly force the unwary under the surface. The Wharfe is allegedly one of the fastest rising rivers that we have in Britain and just a few hours of rain can rapidly transform its delightful sparkling waters into a deadly raging torrent.

The strong flows of the river provided the previous generations who inhabited Upper Wharfedale with a tremendous technical advantage. Powerful water sources could drive powerful mills and from the seventeenth century onwards the development of these mills would bring much prosperity to Wharfedale. One such location lays just a little upstream of me at the village of Addingham.

Low Mill

The present settlement at Low Mill is a peaceful development of very carefully renovated mill cottages. It may look that way now, but it has a fascinating industrial past that provides a microcosm of all that has been both good and bad in British industry over the last two hundred or so years.

We will start our story with two gentlemen who lived during the eighteenth century. John Cunliffe made his living as a cloth maker and John Crockshott was a skilled glazier and wool stapler. These two men formed a business partnership and together purchased some land near to the village of Addingham to build a new cotton textile factory. Their intention was to harness the power of the River Wharfe in order to drive the cotton-looms. In the end Cunliffe and Crockshott did not follow their original plan. During the time that the mill was being constructed the two partners had experimented with manufacturing novel textiles from wool, and were enjoying some success with their ideas. By the time the factory building was completed they had abandoned the idea of cotton textiles and set about manufacturing worsteds instead.

There was a general problem with the manufacturing of worsted textiles at that time. In order to make the highest quality worsteds the fibres have to run straight and parallel to each other and not be allowed to twist. When carried out correctly this results in the production of a much smoother yarn. The final fabric produced then has a quality of quickly returning to its original shape when made into a garment, resulting in a much smarter appearance of the finished clothing. The development work carried out by Cunliffe and Crockshott enabled the process to be carried out very economically and Low Mill quickly became established as the first commercially viable production facility for fine quality worsted cloth.

Despite all of their manufacturing successes Low Mill started to run into financial difficulties. Cockcroft found himself with no option other than to enter into bankruptcy. Cunliffe was in a more fortunate position and was able to call on the financial support of one of his relatives and the factory was able to be saved from the clutches of the bailiffs. Low Mill continued to be successfully run by the family firm of J.Cunliffe and Sons until Jeremiah Horsfall took over the lease in 1824.

Horsfall was a great moderniser and wanted to use the latest available technology wherever possible. He ordered in some new spinning mules from a manufacturer in Manchester with the aim of boosting production at Low Mill. Unfortunately not everyone in those times was so enthusiastic over the introduction of more efficient machinery. None more so than a young man by the name of Ned Ludd who was a factory worker from Nottingham. The introduction of new high productivity equipment was putting thousands of workers out of their traditional jobs leading to severe unemployment. Young Ned and his followers had responded to the loss of jobs by entering the factories and smashing the new machines into pieces. These protesters became more commonly known as "Luddites" after their founder. Ned always carried a sledgehammer that he nicknamed "Great Enoch", and he would defiantly wield his weapon of destruction against the new powerful looms.

Horsfall's consignment of spinning mules had to be delivered overland from Manchester. While in transit the convoy was attacked by a Luddite band led by "Gurt Bill" from Cowling and the spinning mules were completely destroyed. Not content with that, the wreckers decided that they would take further action against the factory that had ordered the tools and set off for Low Mill to do their worst.

Word quickly reached the factory that the protesters were on their way to wreak havoc and the workers prepared their defences. The factory manager had served in the Battle of Waterloo and he was having none of this Luddite lark while he was in charge. Protective iron grills were erected at the windows and the workers prepared themselves for a siege. Low Mill managed to keep the aggressors at bay for a whole day until a detachment of Hussars arrived from Leeds to drive them off. The outer buildings were completely ransacked but the main factory remained intact thanks to the defensive efforts of the villagers. The Hussars stayed on for a few weeks but the Luddites never returned to Low Mill, preferring to concentrate their actions on easier targets. Many other mills throughout England were not so fortunate, and an immense amount of damage was inflicted on the textile industry of the early 19th century by Ned Ludd and his followers.

Undeterred by the attack Horsfall continued to develop his factory using all of the modern aids that he could lay his hands on. In 1827 he built his own gas works so that the factory and the village would benefit from having their own supply. He also introduced a steam-powered mill in 1835 in order to further boost the mill's productivity. Everything seemed to be progressing really well and then, in 1841, Horsfall suddenly stopped trading.

The lease on the factory was taken on by two businessmen William Threlfall and William Seed. They soon ran into financial difficulties and bankruptcy soon followed.

Low Mill was re-opened in 1851 by Samuel Cunliffe-Lister, a descendant of John Cunliffe. Samuel was another one of life's go-getters and piled innovation upon innovation to drive the factory forward. He correctly worked out that the wool combing process was a huge bottleneck in the worsted manufacturing process and altered his production system so that the fibres were carded first. There were no machines available at that time to carry out this work so the enterprising Cunliffe-Lister designed his own device and successfully patented it. Not content with this he then set about developing a process for combing silk, and by 1860 had designed an economically viable method for carrying out this process as well. Finally, in 1878, he invented a power loom for weaving velvet.

The Low Mill factory continued to prosper until the outbreak of the First World War when tariffs started to erode the profitability of the business. The Second World War was to have a far more drastic effect on the use of the mill. When the SU Carburetor factory in Coventry was bombed the production of these important components was moved to Low Mill. Over 1000 workers were taken from Coventry to Yorkshire and housed in Ilkley in a move to keep the important production line going.

After the war ended the carburetor production moved back to Coventry and Low Mill once again reverted to the traditional trade that it knew so well. Initially it was boom time for the factory because the hostilities had caused a considerable shortage of quality textiles and the order books bulged as a consequence. After a short boom-time the orders started to fade away and it became evident that times had changed once more. The old methods and machines were no match for the newly equipped European textile factories and Low Mill found it increasingly difficult to compete in the international marketplace.

The writing was on the wall in big letters. Spinning came to a halt in 1967 and the rest of the factory finally fell silent in 1976. There was a brief renaissance in 1999 when a Norwegian company called StraumUK started to produce scoured wool at the Low Mill site. This venture was unfortunately short-lived and the factory was finally given its death sentence in 2002.

What I can see here now is a lovingly restored and converted residential area overlooking a wonderfully attractive weir. Looking around it hardly seems possible that this was once such a hotbed of the textile industry.

Addingham

The path leaves the river and veers right towards the Parish Church of St. Peter which sits among trees and is surrounded by a stone-walled graveyard. The gravestones are interspersed with clumps of yellow and white daffodils. It is a very pretty location and presents a good photograph opportunity.

One of the first things that strikes the visitor is that looking up at the tower one can see that the clock is unusual in possessing a blue face. This clock is one of several similarly coloured clocks in Yorkshire, and the exact colouring of the face is known as "Pott's

Blue". This unusual feature is the result of the attention to detail of the Leeds-based clock-making company William Potts and Sons. They discovered that gold painted numerals on clock faces stand out far more clearly against a blue background than they do against a traditional black surface.

Addingham is one of those long and spread-out villages that are strung along the road rather than having been built around a central village location. The River Wharfe just touches the eastern edge of the village and I am quickly back to the openness of the riverside pastures.

The next landmark is the small meeting house at Farfield. This is a Friends Meeting House, and is the first of several buildings that were constructed by the members of the Quaker Movement that I will come upon over the next few days. A notice board provides the information that the building is managed by the Historic Chapels Trust and that the original structure dates from 1689. The guidebook tells me that the meeting house has not been in regular use since the 19th century but today there is a builders truck outside and a couple of workmen carrying out some renovations to the roof so it looks as though it is intended to bring it back to serviceable use in the near future.

Fly Fishing on the River Wharfe

At regular intervals along the river I have encountered anglers standing knee-deep in the waters casting their fly-lines in search of their intended quarry. These anglers are seeking either Brown Trout (*Salmo trutta*) or Grayling (*Thymallus thymallus*), both species being native to the River Wharfe. The Wharfe is an excellent angling river throughout most of its length for both the fly fishermen and the coarse fisherman. Fly fishing really comes into its own in the more rapid waters above Ilkley and continues to offer superb sport until the size of the river noticeably declines above the village of Kettlewell.

The River Wharfe is one of England's premier game-fishing rivers and offers the enthusiast a very different challenge to the more delicate chalk-streams that are to be found in southern England. Its southern counterparts have more gentle crystal clear waters, but here the flows are much more powerful. The river is often tinged with a peaty stain that sometimes gives the water more of the appearance of best Yorkshire bitter rather than the gin-clear transparency of a Hampshire stream.

The predominant fish are Brown Trout and Grayling and the features of the river make an ideal habitat for the two species. Waterfalls, springs, cascades and riffles add together to provide high levels of dissolved oxygen, whilst submerged rocks, undercut banks and overhanging vegetation provide protection from bright sunlight and predators.

The brown trout has a very distinctive colouring. Dark-brown spots stand out against a background of scales that start off as a light brassy effect on the back, gradually fading to a light cream colour on the underbelly. Typically the fish caught from the Wharfe will weigh in at between 8oz and 1 ½ lbs. Most of them will probably be towards the bottom of that scale, although no doubt the fisherman will tell you that "the one that got away" was much nearer to the higher limit, and no doubt would have weighed even more if it had not slipped the hook!

Brown Trout spawn late in the year, usually between October and December depending upon local conditions. Spawning fish seek out an area of gravel bed with the ideal size of the stones being that of a garden pea. The female will dig out a shallow trench with her tail and encourage the male to join her in the gulley. After frantic activity the hen fish will lay around 900 eggs for each pound of her bodyweight and these will be fertilised with the male milt. The female will cover the eggs to shield them from the attention of predators. Hatching will occur some three months later. Early stages of life for a trout are highly hazardous and very few eggs will survive the rigours of the five years or so that it takes to become a full-sized trout.

Grayling have a slightly different life-cycle. This fish is programmed to spawn as the days get longer in the period March to June. They are also much faster growing; only taking two years to reach maturity. Known to anglers as "the Lady of the Stream" the grayling is basically a silvery colour, with a slight tinge of metallic-blue. It possesses a large dorsal fin and has a very pronounced upper lip.

The Wharfe contains an abundance of aquatic life that provides a plentiful source of nourishment to the fish. Grubs, nymphs, bloodworm, daphnia, fish-eggs and frogs-spawn are all readily available. These are added to by a host of flying insets that fall or are blown onto the water and become trapped in the surface-film. The skilled angler will try to imitate these ensnared insects with his artificial fly patterns, and use his rod to present the lure to the fish in as natural a manner as possible.

I stop and talk to a couple of anglers who have taken a break and are sitting on the bank munching their sandwiches. It would seem that quite a number of trout had been caught already this morning and that the water conditions were ideal for it to be a very promising day for the fishermen.

Moving on I soon arrived at Bolton Bridge. A blue-painted wooden bench seat stood conveniently by the side of the path where it squeezed past a stone cottage. On the top rear slat there are white painted characters informing me of the distances from the bench for the two end-points of the Dales Way. Thus I learned that I had travelled only 5 ¼ miles from Ilkley and that there are still another 78 ¾ miles to Bowness. There is still a long long way still to go.

Bolton Abbey

Bolton Abbey appears to be a whole world of contradictions. For a start the original ecclesiastical building was not called Bolton Abbey but Bolton Priory. On the other hand the village carries the Abbey suffix. How the two parts first acquired their different names is a matter of some conjecture. One of the more interesting theories is that when the railway first arrived in the valley the station was incorrectly featured in the train timetable as Bolton Abbey by mistake and nobody could ever be bothered to correct it. A far more likely explanation is that the name is the result of a combination of local snobbery and spin-doctoring. In olden times a priory was not deemed to be as impressive or important as an abbey so in a fit of one-upmanship the village decided to promote itself to an Abbey.

A further confusion is that this estate in deepest Yorkshire is actually the residence of the Duke of Devonshire. To compound matters further Bolton Abbey is currently managed as a part of the Chatsworth Estate, which is in Derbyshire.

What is not in any confusion is the sheer natural beauty of this country estate. It is an extremely popular tourist magnet with thousands of visitors flocking to this picturesque part of the Wharfe Valley every weekend. The guidebook informs me that the estate covers 30,000 acres and there are over 80 miles of permissive footpaths that criss-cross within its boundaries.

Today the old priory itself is in ruins, but standing on its mound proudly overlooking the river the remaining stonework still presents a majestic viewpoint. The Priory was founded in 1154 when the land for the building was granted to the Augustinian Order of monks by Lady Alice de Rumily who was the owner of nearby Skipton Castle. Local legend relates that the grant was made to atone for her grief over the death of her son, the "Boy of

Egremont" who allegedly died in the waters of The Strid. This would be a touching little story except for the minor inconvenience that the boy's signature appears on the deeds of endowment to the Priory so we must assume that he was very much alive at the time of the grant.

The black-robed Augustinian monks followed the teachings of St. Augustine (sometimes also referred to as St. Austin) who was born November 13th 354 A.D. in Thagaste, which is the present town of Souk Ahras in Algeria. Augustine had a wide-ranging influence on the philosophies and teachings of the early Christian church. He was the first theologian to propose the concept of original sin and also expounded the notion that there could be such a thing as a "just war" that was not fought purely for wealth, power and greed. His social teachings were based upon the concepts of shared possessions, frugal living, chastity and caring for the sick and destitute.

This particular group of monks had arrived in the Bolton area some two years previously and had begun to build their community at the nearby village of Embsay. The land granted to them by Lady Alice was much more hospitable with the surrounding hills offering shelter from the severe harshness of the bitter Yorkshire winters. Bolton Abbey quickly flourished and swiftly became a major influence on the surrounding area.

It is very difficult for us living in the 21st century to appreciate the lifestyle of a medieval monk. In our minds we tend to think only of lines of tonsured men trudging head-bowed and silent through the cloisters on their way to endless vespers. For the vast majority of monks this was not their experience at all. OK, so they did spend many hours in prayer and contemplation, but so did many other people during that period in our history. Monasteries were much more diverse and important to the community in medieval times than we could ever imagine with our modern outlook on life.

To begin with the monasteries were the only providers of education in early times. Only the learned scholars of Oxford and Cambridge could come close to the knowledge held by the monks. There was also no medical care, hospitals, local surgeries or family doctors to be found anywhere. The only providers of any form of care services for the sick were the monks and nuns of the monasteries.

The monasteries were also the great chroniclers of their times. Without their meticulous records we would have no written evidence for any of the events that have occurred in our history. Books were painstakingly written and copied by hand. It could be an entire lifetime's work for one monk to copy just one solitary book. Whole teams of monks would spend their days hunched over desks and there are many examples of their illuminated manuscripts that can be seen in museums throughout the country.

Don't believe all of that total poverty lark either. The individual monks had very few possessions themselves, but their monasteries were loaded with riches. Once established the monastery would generate its own income from agriculture, milling and brewing. They had a nice little trick that in addition to their own efforts they were able to encourage the local peasants to assist them in their labours without giving any payment in return. This is because in those days the influence of the church was so powerful that most of the people considered it to be their duty to help by working two days a week for nothing for the church's benefit. Not only that, but the villagers would then give 10% of everything else they earned to the church as well! It is from this last practice that we derive the word "tithe" meaning a payment. It was originally used as a term for the payment of "one tenth" of a person's income that was taken by the church.

A further source of income that was exploited by the monasteries was in the provision of bridges and crossings. Many bridges the length and breadth of Britain were first constructed by the religious houses. Then what do you think that the monasteries did when the crossings were completed? That's right; they charged a whacking great toll to everyone who wanted to use them.

It would be remiss to leave the impression that life for a medieval monk was all a "nice little earner". Conditions at times could be very harsh, and the erratic Yorkshire weather would very much decide the success or failure of their crops which in turn would determine whether the next few months were going to be ones of feast or famine. There were also no conditions in those days that could not be made many times worse by the gangs of marauding Scots who would regularly journey south in search of loot and plunder.

The Priory at Boston prospered until 1539 when Henry VIII ordered it to be closed as part of his campaign to remove the power of the large religious houses during what has become known as the "Dissolution of the Monasteries".

The main priory was allowed to continue to be used as a parish church, but the remaining buildings were stripped bare and their roofs removed. Erosion by the elements soon started to crumble some of the walls, and in a typical Yorkshire "waste not – want not" fashion many of the stones were recycled and put to good use in the construction of many of the cottages throughout the valley.

The Priory Church is dedicated to St. Mary and St. Cuthbert and has been lovingly restored over the recent centuries. It is well worth the short diversion from the Dales Way Path just to admire the magnificent stained glass windows and to view the wonderful paintings of the East Wall.

The restoration work commenced in the 19th century under the direction of the 5th Duke of Devonshire. The Duke had been impressed with the displays of the designer Augustus Pugin at the Great Exhibition of 1851 and commissioned him to design the south window for the church. On a bright day the sun's rays light up the window into a glorious multichromatic display of colour. There are 36 pictures depicting the story of the life of Christ from Annunciation through to Resurrection. Other stained glass windows include that of a royal head which is alleged to be that of Edward III who was a major benefactor of the Priory during his reign. There is also the "Cuthbert Window" that shows St. Cuthbert, when he was the Bishop of Lindisfarne, cradling the head of the martyred St. Oswald

After the completion of the stained glass features the highly-regarded architect George Street was commissioned to redesign the interior. This consisted of new pews, sanctuary and a font. The work was completed in 1867.

The East Wall of the church was rebuilt in 1880. Local artist Thomas Bottomley was instructed to decorate the wall. With the aid of his apprentice, R.A.Greenwood, Bottomley created an impressive display of flowers and symbols. The frieze is a series of panels with each individual piece showing a flower standing above a symbol.

More recently, during the 1970's, the West Tower that had been slowly disintegrating for over 400 years was finally restored. A new roof was constructed, a floor installed, and the windows were glazed. I use the word restored, but in truth the Tower had never been completed in the first place. Henry VIII had caused the initial building of the tower to be abandoned by his decree of dissolution and the work had never been restarted.

Whilst the ruined priory undoubtedly has its own form of beauty the major attraction for the many visitors who flock here is the wonderful scenery of the countryside. The river flows serenely through the grassy pastures and ahead of me I can see glorious broad-leaved woodlands covering either side of the valley.

The path crosses the river at a stone bridge, but it is much more fun to use the stepping stones spread between the banks. It is a good-sized step to cover some of the gaps, and the water swirls around the stones scouring some holes in the river-bed that look particularly hungry for the misplaced foot of the careless rock-hopper. The stones are no place for the timid. Such is the popularity of this method of transferring from one bank to the other that a more-or-less continuous line of people constantly forms along the length of the stones. When one person hesitates and the doubt creeps into their minds about wisdom of taking the next step the whole line comes to a halt and stares at the apprehensive figure at the front. There is no possibility of turning back because all of the platforms behind them are occupied. After a few seconds the hesitant step is taken with a slight waving of arms in a cartoon style "tightrope-balancing" action. You can sense the relief from several stones back when they stand upright on the next stone without getting a wet shoe. The star-of-the-moment continues on their way no doubt feeling just that bit more elated from their thrill-seeking experience. The kids all love it and race over the bridge to join the back of the line to do it all over again. Simple pleasures.

The path weaves between the trees gradually climbing up the lower slopes of the valley. At this time of the year the trees are not yet fully in leaf and the path affords the best views of the Abbey ruins and the river below. The white ruined arch of the large window stands defiantly upright as a focus point against the background of green hills, while the river flows along the valley floor, its surface reflecting the sun.

I continue along this route mostly looking across the valley and not where I am walking and I literally stumble upon the celebrated "Money Tree". Unfortunately, before anybody becomes too excited, this is not a freak of nature that defies the traditional saying "money doesn't grow on trees" but a man-made decoration. Over the years many passing walkers have thought that they would make their own contributions to the ambience of the surroundings by hammering coins into the bark of a fallen trunk. Continual exposure to the elements has left most of the coins in a sorry state and very few have any clear markings remaining. However there must be a considerable weight of coinage tightly wedged into the crevices and cracks of the old trunk.

After the "money tree" the path descends to the river and takes me over a footbridge and I find myself at the very welcoming Cavendish Pavilion. This spot is fair teeming with visitors enjoying the countryside and I consider myself lucky to find an empty table outside the tea-room for lunch.

Embsay and Bolton Steam Railway

Phhyshhhtickuff - Phhyshhhtickuff -Phhyshhhtickuff!

We are all kids really when we are given half the chance. Only five miles away there is a personal appearance by a well-loved character from my childhood and I am literally going to be transported back to that wonderful time.

Ivor the Engine is here!

The little green engine is visiting Embsay Station today and I just can't miss it. Will he still be driven by "Jones the Steam"? Will he be patiently waiting for the whistle and flag of "Dai Station" to set him off on his way? And for the real aficionados will "Idris the Dragon" still be living in his firebox?

The Embsay and Bolton Steam Railway is operated by volunteer enthusiasts and is a real joy to travel on. For only £8 return the visitor can experience the wonders of steam travel, and for only a small extra supplement can travel in the exclusive "First Class" carriage which has comfortable armchairs and highly polished woodwork.

The history of the railway has that familiar ring to it. The original railway between Ilkley and Skipton was opened in 1888 and was a part of the Midland Railway Company. Inevitably as these things tended to happen the line was recommended for closure along with the rest of the Wharfedale railway system by the infamous Beeching Report of the 1960's. Local opposition campaigns raged against the plans but the line was closed in 1965 and the rails lifted. Inspired by other groups of railway enthusiasts who were successfully re-opening stretches of line the Embsay and Grassington Railway Preservation Society was formed in 1968.

The members started to buy up lengths of the trackbed and also built the engineering sheds at Embsay for the restoration of locomotives and rolling stock. The line was extended in stages until finally in May 1998 the railway from Embsay to Bolton Abbey was officially opened.

At the time of writing the assets of the railway are very impressive. There are 19 steam locomotives, 13 diesel locomotives, 30 carriages and 35 assorted wagons. This is not to mention two stations, a halt, signal boxes, bridges and a whole panoply of memorabilia that is dotted around the stations and carriages.

From the Abbey it is about a half-hour walk to the reconstructed Bolton Abbey Station. When the station was purchased by the Steam Railway in the mid-1990's the original buildings were beyond any hope of restoration so there was no alternative than to rebuild from scratch. A brand new station was built from timber in the style of the original buildings. Many businesses supplied materials free of charge and the construction company Robert McAlpine Ltd carried out the work without accepting payment. Yorkshire Television's "Action Time" programme also gave considerable assistance to the project.

Back in the hey-day of the railways in the early part of the twentieth century the station at Bolton Abbey would be extremely busy on Bank Holidays. Special excursion trains were run from all over Yorkshire as people fled the cities for a few brief hours of relaxation in the countryside. It was not unusual for 40,000 passengers to use Bolton Abbey on these occasions.

Not so many people at the station today as the green locomotive "Monkton" pulls the train alongside the platform. In common with many of the steam locomotives on this railway "Monkton" previously worked as a colliery engine, in this case at NCB North Gawber Colliery at Barnsley. For the benefit of train spotters "Monkton" has a works number of 3788 and has a wheel arrangement of 0-6-0ST. The cylinder size is 18 inches and the locomotive was built by Hunslet in 1953.

There will be a delay while the engine is uncoupled and transferred via a system of points to the opposite end of the train for the return journey. Soon we are ready to go and with a blast of the steam-whistle we are away.

The train puffs its way sedately through the Yorkshire countryside. The views from the carriages must be much the same as they would have been many years ago. Lambs are gamboling in the fields and the green hillsides are interspersed with small quarries, their stone faces glinting in the spring sunlight.

There is a short interlude at Stoneacre Loop where the train stops to let its working companion for the day to pass in the opposite direction. The volunteer railwaymen impeccably follow the strict safety procedures where a metal loop is passed over to the signalman to signify that the track is clear before the points are changed. It is an old system dating back to the early days of the railways but it is still a very effective manual safety system to prevent two trains finding themselves heading towards each other on the same piece of track.

When the train pulls into Embsay Station I can see Ivor waiting in his siding, surrounded by excited youngsters. They are all clutching their "Ivor" goodie bags and "Ivor" commemorative flags. Plenty of dads around too, while the mothers are usually to be found giving their men-folk that special indulgent look that only the female of the species can give; the look that says "What on earth do you find so fascinating about an old green kettle on wheels choking me half to death and making my clothes smelly, but if it makes you happy......".

Embsay Station has a bookshop. So does Euston, but the London Terminus does not have anything like the range of books that Embsay has. According to the advertising blurb this is a transport bookshop. However, can you hazard a guess which form of transport features the most? There are literally thousands of books on railways. OK there are also several hundreds of books on other forms of locomotion but it is the trains that rule the roost. I asked the manager how many different titles there were and he informed me that at the last stocktaking there were over 4,000 but they had a few more available now because it was approaching the peak tourist season. I introduced myself and we chatted for a while about the difficulties of getting specialist books published and he promised to stock this one when I have it finished.

There is scarcely time to scratch the surface of the shop contents before the next train leaves. I grab a couple of books on the history of the Embsay Railway and scurry off to claim my seat for the return journey to Bolton Abbey and resume my acquaintance with the Dales Way.

The Bodger

A short walk from the Cavendish Pavilion I come across a small crowd gathered at a rickety-looking canvas shelter. Closer investigation reveals that I have come across the workplace of a man who practices an old traditional craft using similar tools to those used by his predecessors thousands of years ago.

Richard Law is a traditional craftsman who loves his work, and also loves sharing his ideals and creations with others. Be careful how you interpret the next sentence before you reach the wrong conclusion. Richard is a bodger and this shelter is his hovel.

Words can often be used and taken for the wrong meaning and for many people the words "bodger" and "botcher" are the same thing. Even the "Concise Oxford English Dictionary" refers the inquisitive reader to turn from "bodger" to "botcher" to obtain a definition. The two are quite different, but it seems that common usage has now brought them together which is a great pity because in the true traditional forms they are at opposite ends of the scale. A botched job is one that is incompetently performed and inevitably results in a very shoddy piece of work being produced. It is believed to derive from the medieval word "botch" which was used to describe an unsightly carbuncle or boil. On the other hand a "bodged" job is one performed by somebody who utilises readily available materials to carry out a task and results in a perfectly serviceable product.

So taking all that in what does a person who enthusiastically calls themselves a "Bodger" actually do? In simple terms he takes unseasoned greenwood and transforms it into useful objects by traditional methods. The term was originally coined in the furniture industry in the Chiltern Hills of the High Wycombe area. A bodger would set up his workshop in the beech woods and turn the greenwood into chair legs and stretchers. The area that the bodger utilised as his workshop was known as his hovel.

The bodger would typically begin his work by purchasing some suitable trees from the estate. He would then set up his hovel, usually a lean-to type of shelter covered with material such as the one by the path at Bolton Abbey. Although it was referred to as a hovel this was generally not where the bodger lived, merely his place of work. Normally the craftsman would live in the local village and walk to his workshop. It was far less effort to take the workshop to the source of timber than the other way around.

Once the bodger had established his hovel he could set about his craft. A tree would be selected and felled. In the beech woodlands of the Chilterns this would have traditionally been a beech tree, but here in Bolton Abbey there are many different woods to choose from.

The next step would be to cut the tree and its branches into logs that would enable billets to be prepared for the final parts of the process. These logs would be slightly longer than the length of the finished product.

Phase two was to split the logs into thinner strips for working on the lathe. Traditionally this was done in two parts. Firstly the logs would be split using an axe and a wedge through the cut end of the log. Secondly the split log would be fixed to the shave-horse, or trestle, where the bodger would shave down the wood to a more workable diameter to form his billet. This was achieved by using a draw-knife, which was a giant spoke-shave that the bodger would pull towards him and slice quickly along the grain. Using the draw-knife is much quicker than using a lathe because the greenwood slices much more easily with the grain, whereas using the lathe would cut against the grain.

Finally the bodger would use his pole-lathe and chisels to finish the work. The pole-lathe has a real rustic appearance and to the casual observer it is all a little bit "Heath-Robinson", but after a few moments thought it is actually quite a clever construction. The long pole is angled into the air and acts as a tensioning spring. A chord is fixed to the free end of the pole and is wrapped several times around the billet before being fixed to a treadle. Depressing the treadle pulls the chord and in turns rotates the billet. The treadle is then depressed the other way and the billet will turn in the opposite direction. The craftsman would then use his chisels to pare down the billet into the final shape. Frequent sharpening is required to keep the chisels effective because unseasoned greenwood blunts the edge far quicker than is the case with properly seasoned timber.

The chair legs would then be stacked for seasoning, and then taken to the furniture factory to be sold. Most of the work of the traditional Chilterns bodgers was to fashion the legs and stretchers for the classic "Windsor Chair" that used to be so popular.

Richard is not so specific in his output, and literally turns his hand to many different products. The area around his hovel is choc-a-bloc with bird-tables, stools, ladders, benches and almost anything you could think of that you could possibly make from wood. Many pieces are made to order and Richard is always delighted to discuss individual requirements.

There are wood shavings everywhere as you might expect. This provided the inspiration for name of the website www.flyingshavings.co.uk which features more details of Richard's work, including pictures and a regular blog showing the stages involved in the creation of his latest works. Richard can usually be found working here Sunday to Thursday, or you may come across him doing demonstrations at one of the many local shows in the Yorkshire area.

The Strid

The next half hour of my walk will be the most crowded section of the path that I will encounter on my journey. The woodland paths that wind through Strid Wood are extremely popular with visitors and are always busy. Today being a fine spring Saturday it seems to be particularly congested and my progress is going to be slow. People are irresistibly drawn to the combination of broad-leaved trees, rocky outcrops and cascading waters of the steep-sided valley.

In 1985 the Strid Wood was declared a Site of Special Scientific Interest and it is easy to see why. Strid Wood Conservation Area houses a wealth of natural wonders. The trees themselves for a magnificent shady canopy composed mainly of beech and sycamore. They have all been here for quite some time, the largest being around 300 years old.

A rare feature of the woodland is that it provides an ideal environment for the native sessile oak. This variety of the oak tree prefers the naturally wetter acidic soils that are found at Bolton Abbey. It can be distinguished from its arboreal relatives by the lack of a stalk supporting the acorns. Strid Wood contains the greatest concentration of oak woodland in the whole Yorkshire Dales National Park.

Bird watchers can discover over sixty different species flying through the treetops, and there are also five different species of bat living here.

The botanists will find their appetites whetted by a wide range of treats. Carpets of bluebells are everywhere and are a very obvious attraction, but less conspicuously lurking among the tree trunks and rocks there are literally hundreds of different species of mosses, lichens, fungi and liverworts.

The river here is considerably narrower than it is at the Priory, rushing through deep channels in the rock. There are many small waterfalls and races to attract the eye, but there is one in particular that gives the area its name. After twenty minutes of walking from the café I join the crowd standing above the thundering waters of The Strid.

The Strid could be described as a small waterfall but that does not do it justice. Being barely a yard wide, only a few yards long and with a drop in height of only a few feet it does not sound very impressive. However when you have all of the waters of the River Wharfe thundering through this small gap in the rocks it becomes something much more spectacular.

Deep and narrow channels in the rocks have been gouged out by the abrasive actions of stones swirling in the torrid waters. Over many thousands of years this action has worn away the softer rocks into potholes that can be seen scattered along the riverbed when the river is running low. Over the ages some of these holes became joined together and eventually became narrow chasms. While there are several similar features to be found along this section of the Wharfe the most impressive by far is The Strid.

At first view The Strid may appear relatively innocuous. Allegedly it was originally named The Strid because it is just a man's stride in breadth, but it would be a very foolhardy person who attempted this feat. Stop for a while and ponder the logic of what we have here. The whole of the River Wharfe, fed from countless mountain streams from England's largest range of hills is being forced through a tiny gap in the rocks. The pressure of the water must be immense. Even as I approach, the roar of the water seems to shout out its warning that this piece of water is not to be messed with. According to the "Yorkshire Dales" website there has never been a recorded instance of anyone surviving a fall into the thundering jets. These jets have over time eroded the rocks to an incredible depth, and the chasm is currently estimated to be about 30 feet (9m) from top to bottom. Under the surface are more unseen potholes and channels that have been carved out of the rocks. It can be a very dangerous place

Barden Tower

Moving upstream of The Strid the footpath climbs up the slope of the gorge and provides an elevated viewpoint to the waters below. After a few minutes it steadily works its way back to the riverside. Gradually the trees decrease in number until I find myself out of the woodlands and into open countryside. An attractive old bridge stands ahead, seemingly in the middle of nowhere. Three stone arches span the river and the top of the bridge has a straight castellated parapet. It seems an elaborate and expensive footbridge and I reach the conclusion that it must be a "folly" put here primarily for aesthetic purposes. My later researches revealed that far from being a folly there is a very good reason for it being here. The bridge was originally not for transport as we would know it, but was constructed by the Bradford Water Company as an aqueduct to carry water from Nidderdale to the city of Bradford.

Half-hidden among the trees are the box-shaped ruins of Barden Tower which was once the principal hunting lodge of the old Forest of Barden. Barden Tower had existed as a hunting lodge since the early 11th century and owned by the Clifford family, the Lord of Skipton. The ruins that I can see today are the remains of a small castle that was constructed in the 15th century by Henry Clifford, Lord of Skipton. Clifford much preferred to live by the side of the River Wharfe rather than in his ancestral home at Skipton. Henry Clifford was a popular landowner, and was affectionately known as "The Shepherd Lord". This was not only an allusion to the way he looked after his local villagers, but also to the time that he spent being nurtured and protected by a shepherd in his childhood.

Medieval politics were very complex, and the chicanery and double-dealing would have done credit to Machiavelli himself. No wonder that William Shakespeare was able to draw on those times for the plots of many of his plays. So I am not even going to try and explain how it came about that "Butcher" Clifford the 9th Lord of Skipton, in the County of Yorkshire, was fighting for the Lancastrian Red Rose at the Battle of Towton on the 14th of March 1461, but he was. I expect that he ultimately wished that he wasn't because he was killed during that particular altercation. Clifford's lands were seized by the young Edward IV. Lady Clifford, fearing that the Yorkists would kill her young son Henry, sent him away to live with a shepherd at Threlkeld, near Keswick.

The Yorkists were defeated at the Battle of Bosworth Field (1485) and the Lancastrian Henry Tudor (Henry VII) was acclaimed as King. The new King restored the ownership of Barden Tower to Henry Clifford who developed the present castle. The accompanying Priest's House was added in the early 16th century to accommodate Clifford's favourite priest. The Priest's House has recently been converted to a restaurant.

The original Tower proved to be none too resilient to the Yorkshire weather, and it had to be restored by Lady Anne Clifford in the late sixteen fifties. A visit to view the Tower at closer quarters necessitates taking a short diversion from the main path, but a few minutes walk soon brings me back to the riverside and I can enjoy a steady stroll along the bank side to Barden Bridge.

The Barden Triangle

Barden Bridge in an impressive elegant bridge possessing three high arches and angled buttresses. It was rebuilt in 1676 after its predecessor was washed away in heavy floods. The floods that year must have been an extremely devastating, because the bridges at Kettlewell, Burnsall, Bolton, Ilkley and Otley were also washed away in the same deluge.

The bridge marks the end of the Bolton Abbey Estate. It is a popular area for picnickers with a car park in the final meadow and more parking spaces for vehicles by the roadside. According to the map I have walked a little over four miles through the Estate although I have taken several deviations to explore the surrounding areas. In retrospect it has not been far, but it has been packed with interesting things to see and ponder over. As pleasant as it has been so far, I need to put those thoughts behind me because I will need to concentrate all my attention on the route ahead.

I have to keep my wits about me because I am now entering the area known as the "Barden Triangle". This area of Upper Wharfedale is said to possess mysterious magical powers. Barden Bridge marks the southern end of this supernatural environment. The enchanted sites include Elbolton Hill, Trollers Gill and Dibbles Bridge.

Elbolton Hill near Thorpe is regarded by local legend as the home of the fairies. The hill is part of the small range known as the Cracope Reef Knolls. These hills were fashioned out of the remnants of a prehistoric coral reef. It is hard to imagine that this by inference would have to mean that at some time in the history of our planet the surrounding countryside would have been submerged under a shallow tropical sea.

Trollers Gill is in nearby Appletreewick and is a sharp narrow ravine at the head of Trollerdale. The multitude of nooks and crannies of Trollers Gill are alleged to be the home of aggressive troll-like sprites, who hurl boulders at anyone passing through the ravine and then devour the flesh of the unfortunate victim. Fortunately Trollers Gill is well away from my intended route so being stoned by sprites is a risk that I will not have to take today.

Dibbles Bridge, so local legend has it, was built by the devil in return for a favour carried out for him by a local shoemaker. This brings up the inevitable question which brings a smile to my face. Does this bridge really belong to the devil, or is it cobblers?

If all of these horrifying myths and legends are not enough to unsettle the nervous traveler there is the added danger of unintentionally stumbling across the terrifying "Barguest". This spectral beast is reputed to haunt the area around Appletreewick and is alleged to be a huge fierce-looking hound. This canine ghost is said to have huge terrifying eyes that are as big as saucers, and a great cavernous mouth lined with giant fangs. An encounter with the Barguest is considered to be the forewarning of an untimely death.

Hopefully I will be able to make my way to Grassington without a major incident and be able to exit this potentially doom-laden triangle without experiencing any supernatural influences.

Appletreewick and William Craven

The small and curiously-named village of Appletreewick becomes visible to my right. I have been told that the local dialect pronounces the name as "Ap'trick" which makes it much less of a mouthful.

Appletreewick is virtually a one-street settlement dating back to medieval times. The village was originally noted for its sheep, the local lead mines and a somewhat local speciality for growing onions. All of this was to change in the early 17th century when a local lad from a poor family set off to seek his fortune in London Town and worked his way up in the world to achieve the distinction of being the Lord Mayor of London. Appletreewick is the birthplace of William Craven who enjoys the reputation of being the "Yorkshire Dick Whittington" and a major inspiration for the rags-to-riches fairy tale.

William was born into poverty in Appletreewick around 1548, and when still a boy travelled to London to be apprenticed to a merchant tailor. It would be nice to think that he had tied up all his belongings in a white-spotted red handkerchief, slung the package over his shoulder on a stout stick and strode down the earlier version of the M1 accompanied by his cat. Inevitably he would have stopped by a milepost, looked sideways at the cat, and then loudly slapping his thigh exclaiming "It's a long way to London, Puss!" before striding on again towards his destination.

The young William must have worked extremely hard at learning his trade, for at the age of twenty-one he became a fully-fledged member of the Merchant Tailors Guild. This was a remarkable achievement in itself for one so young, let alone a person originating from a humble background. Craven's creations were extremely popular with the members of London Society and he soon developed a clientele that was sufficiently numerous to enable him to set up his own business. His fashions grew in popularity and consequently the poor boy from the dales became extremely wealthy. In 1594 Craven was one of the founding contributors to St. John's College, Oxford University. However high he had risen in society William Craven never forgot his own humble origins and he was determined to provide the resources to aid the prospects of his former villagers. In 1601 Craven founded the Grammar School at Burnsall, a short distance up the Wharfe valley from his home village, so enabling local boys to rise above their lowly station and further their aspirations.

William Craven married a society lady, Elizabeth Whitmore, and together they produced five children, Elizabeth, Mary, William, John and Thomas. The young William married the sister of Charles I and later became Baron Craven of Hampstead Marshall (Berkshire) and also held the title of 1st Earl of Craven.

The riches generated from the successful tailoring business enabled Craven to enter into the realm of politics. In 1600 he was elected Alderman of Bishopsgate and only a year later he became Sherriff of London. The recently crowned King James I awarded Craven a knighthood in 1603, and to make the rags-to-riches tale complete, in 1610 William Craven became the Lord Mayor of London.

William Craven died in July 1618, and has a long lasting memorial in his home village with the local pub named in his honour, the "Craven Arms". As may be expected from its association with this extraordinary man this is no ordinary village pub, but a thriving enterprise with its own annual music festival in April and beer festival in October.

The churlish may want to point out that there actually was a Lord Mayor by the name of Richard Whittington. Well, yes there was. Whittington was Mayor of London in 1397, 1398, 1406 and 1419, around two hundred years before William Craven. Note that Whittington was actually Mayor of London four times, not three as is generally believed to be the case. The first time he held the office he was appointed to the position by Richard II following the untimely death of the previous Lord Mayor. However Richard Whittington was a wealthy man to start with so as eminent as his reputation was for being a highly trusted and respected individual he was not an ideal candidate for a "poor country boy made good" fairy story. The traditional tale of Dick Whittington as we now know it seems to have originated in the early part of the 17th century so it would seem a reasonable conclusion that the two stories became somewhat mixed together. By combining the stories of Craven with those of Whittington we can conjure up the "feel-good" tale of a poor-boy made good and everyone can live happily ever after. If you are not convinced by that analysis let me apply one of my rules of life. "Never let the facts get in the way of a good story".

Burnsall

Burnsall is one of the prettiest places in the whole of the Yorkshire Dales and is known to the locals as "Bonnie Burnsa". It was probably an old Norse settlement with the name originating as a derivative of Bjorns Hall. The village today is a real tourist honeypot.

The first view I have of Burnsall is of the elegant five-arched stone bridge that spans the sparkling waters of the River Wharfe. Beside the bridge stands a row of wonderful limestone houses with the tower of St Wilfred's Church rising above their rooftops. The village nestles in the valley with green hills rising to shelter it on either side. It really is an inviting setting, and the village calls me towards its limestone buildings. This is one of those classic views that many people will be familiar with without knowing where exactly it is. The scene appears on the covers of many books and maps of the Yorkshire Dales, as well as being a regular feature on calendars.

St Wilfred's Church dates its origins back to the 11th century and is a Grade I listed building. The front view is set off nicely by a fine old lych gate leading to the churchyard. Next to the church is the very attractive old grammar school that I have previously related was originally founded by William Craven to educate local boys so that they could improve their prospects and aspire to greater things. The building is now the home of the local primary school so continuing Craven's legacy to his home village.

It is a bright day today and the village and the riverside meadows are packed with visitors. As crowded as it is today this will be a mere sprinkling compared to the crowds who will throng here for the annual Burnsall Feast Sports that are held every August.

The sports date back to Elizabethan times and were originally held to celebrate the Feast of St Wilfred. The official day of St Wilfred is the first Sunday after August 12th, and the sports are traditionally held on the first Saturday after that.

The annual event has evolved into a massive village fair with all kinds of stalls and activities going on. Sports and races provide the major feature and the highlight of the day is the great fell race. According to local tales this race originated in 1870 with a discussion over a few beers in the Red Lion. As the evening progressed and the effects of the ale started to work their wonders one of the participants in the discussion, Tom Weston, decided that it would be a good idea to test the suitability of the course by running it himself on that very moonlit night. As you do.

Which he did.

Stark naked.

The adult race has been run over that same course ever since, although these days (probably much to the disappointment of the local ladies) the participants tend to wear modern running attire.

Loup Scar

The path northwards from Burnsall is extremely popular with walkers and today is no exception. The well-maintained path clings tightly to the side of the river, following every twist and turn. I soon come to view the feature on the opposite bank known as Loup Scar. This is a white limestone buttress standing over the rapids and pools of the river. It makes quite magnificent scenery and it is somewhat a pity that there has to be so many people around to impose upon the natural wonder.

It is a great pity that there were not so many people swarming around here on a particular day in 1766 for if there had been then there would have been plenty of witnesses to a foul murder.

Tom Lee was a rather unsavoury character with a well-deserved reputation for violence and drunkenness. Lee was a blacksmith who operated his forge in the nearby village of Grassington. It was here at Loup Scar that Tom Lee unsuccessfully attempted to dispose of the body of a local physician, by the name of Doctor Petty, in the deep pools of the River Wharfe.

Doctor Petty had outraged Lee by telling him in no uncertain manner to mend his drunken ways. This incident occurred while both men were drinking in the Kilnsley Inn which is located a few miles further upstream above Grassington. The ever-volatile Lee became incandescent with rage over this affront to his dignity and in his alcohol-fuelled rage decided that Petty must be shown who was boss. Lee lay in wait for Dr Petty at the entrance to Grass Wood. When the good doctor passed that way on his journey home the aggrieved Lee sprang out in ambush from his hiding place and brutally beat him to death. Lee desperately attempted to hide the doctor's body in the river at Loup Scar but his efforts at concealment were in vain, for the body was soon discovered.

All of the accusing fingers immediately pointed to Tom Lee, but the forces of law were unable to obtain a conviction. Tom Lee was tried not once, but twice, each time a verdict of "not guilty" being returned by the jury. However, the incident had not changed Lee's character one little bit and after yet another drinking session he boasted to his young apprentice Jack Sharp about the way he had dealt with the disrespect shown to him by Doctor Petty. The apprentice became increasingly concerned that he could now be accused of being a possible accessory to the injustice of the trials. After some while Sharp's troubled conscience caused him to reveal all that he knew to the authorities and he turned King's Evidence against Lee.

The third trial finally found Tom Lee guilty of murder and he was sentenced to be hanged at the entrance to Grass Wood near to where the foul deed had been committed. The site of "Lee's Smithy" in Grassington is marked with a plaque on the wall and is presently used as an art gallery.

Hebden and Linton Falls

The Hebden Suspension Bridge is one of the more interesting crossings over the River Wharfe. It was constructed in 1885 by local blacksmith William Bell to ease the journey of workers between the village of Thorpe and the cotton and corn mills located at Hebden.

The bridge is narrow, only sufficient for one person to cross in either direction. Today this has resulted in a build-up of walkers on either side patiently waiting for their turn to cross. The construction is of wood, suspended by wrapped-steel cables supported from concrete towers on either bank. Everyone can pretend that they are Indiana Jones crossing narrow bridges in the wilds!

It is fun to observe the different behaviours of the people ahead as they make their first steps on to the wooden slats. Some are very hesitant while others take supreme delight in bouncing their way across making the bridge sway from side to side with their enthusiastic movements.

At low water there is a series of stepping stones that provide an alternative crossing, but this is one of those rare occasions where crossing by the bridge provides much more fun.

The village of Hebden lies just off the Dales Way and makes a pleasant diversion. The pathway to the village is well marked from the bridge and it takes about twenty minutes. Excellent refreshments are provided by "The Clarendon Hotel" which makes the diversion very worthwhile. The menu board looks so mouth-watering that with my B&B only a couple of miles away it seems that fate has decreed that I must book a table and return for an evening meal later. My recommendation is that before an evening meal here you only require a very light lunch. The starters are the size of most main courses and the main courses can be staggering!

Hebden is featured in the Domesday Book where it goes by the name of Hebedene. The name is derived from Old English from either Heope meaning rose-hip or Heopa which signifies a bramble. The suffix den is from dene which is the Old English word for valley.

During the nineteenth century Hebden was an industrial village. The main sources of employment in Hebden were cotton mills and corn mills. Hebden was also the home for many miners who were employed in the lead-mines on nearby Grassington Moor.

I retrace my steps back to the suspension bridge to resume the Dales Way path. The path follows a track passing through an avenue of horse-chestnut trees. A lovely shady walk and I should imagine that this section is popular with the local children during the conker season. After a few minutes enjoying the canopy of the trees I am back to the open pastures making for the Linton Falls and the isolated church of St.Michael and All Angels. The church and falls are truthfully closer to Grassington than they are to Linton, but that is by the by.

Standing in splendid isolation on the opposite bank the church of St.Michael and All Angels is much photographed, making it a key focal point of the landscape. The church has a relatively low profile compared to other churches I have passed today, possessing a short stubby bell-tower. What it lacks in height it makes up for in area for it must have one of the greatest floor areas of any Yorkshire parish church. The falls are also extremely photogenic with a very popular shot being of the stepping stones that cross the river just below the falls keeping the falls in the background. The stones are only suitable for use at low water levels, and then only for the brave or foolhardy.

Linton Mill closed in 1959 and has now been converted to housing. A bridge leads across the river to the old mill and church.

I continue to follow the path over the waterside meadows and the stone bridge at Grassington gradually comes into view. The bridge is flat with four large arches spanning the river and two smaller arches on the edge of the bank, one at either end.

Grassington Bridge marks the end of my journey for the day. It is also goodbye for a while to the bubbly River Wharfe. The next part of my journey will take me up the sides of the valley and across the limestone features on the top of Grassington Moor before descending to pick up the River Wharfe again at the charming village of Kettlewell.

DAY TWO

GRASSINGTON TO BECKERMONDS

15.9 MILES

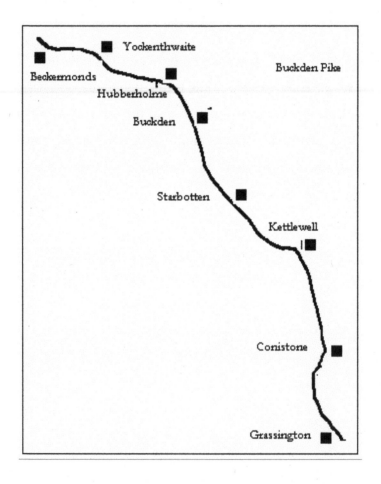

Grassington

Grassington can be considered to be the "capital" of the Upper Wharfedale area. It is the size of place that falls into that category which can be described either as a large village or a small town and would be well described both times.

There have been settlements at Grassington throughout the ages, and there is sufficient evidence to show that the area site has been regularly inhabited for around 4000 years, dating back to 2000BC. The surroundings are rich in archaeological heritage. Bronze Age burial mounds, Celtic homesteads and Roman farms have all been discovered in the locality. Who knows what other artifacts lurk under the surface still waiting their turn to be discovered?

The area was at one time notable for its arable crops. The Celts and Norse both established farms here. During the Roman occupation the conditions were even considered suitable to support the growing of grain. The Domesday Book records that there were over 300 acres allocated to arable farmland. A market charter was awarded to Grassington in 1282 so it seemed to be developing quite nicely as a trading post as well.

However, it was not to be agriculture that spurred the growth of Grassington, it was the rich seams of lead ore that could be mined from the sides of the valley. In the 15th century George Clifford, Earl of Cumberland became Lord of the Manor and set about exploiting the abundant local availability of the mineral. Clifford brought in skilled miners from Derbyshire and Cornwall to extract the ore, and the mining industry in Grassington started to dominate the local economy.

In 1750 the lead-mining industry experienced a further boost when the Duke of Devonshire married one of the Clifford heiresses and as a consequence also became the Lord of Grassington. He was responsible for the construction of a new smelting mill that expanded the industry even more.

All of the prosperity from the mining industry did have its drawbacks. The miners were mostly hardened and unruly characters, and their hobbies all seemed to be concentrated on drinking, cockfighting and bearbaiting. Stories have it that the Grassington constabulary were the first police force in Britain that needed to be routinely armed in order to keep the boisterous populace at bay.

The boom years for the lead mining industry in Grassington were between the early 17th century and early 19th century. After this the industry started to decline, and by the 1870's the decline had turned into a slump and many people deserted the area in search of making a living elsewhere. There was a short-lived attempt to develop a textile industry to generate employment for the local residents, but by the time the century had turned the local population had dropped to around 300.

The area was saved by the coming of the railway to nearby Threshfield situated on the opposite bank of the River Wharfe. Grassington became a place where people could venture into the countryside to escape form the cities of Leeds and Bradford. Some people were fortunate enough to be able to afford to move to the countryside and commute to the cities for their work.

Grassington village has since thrived, and today it is full of hotels, cafes and shops catering for the tourist industry. The main focus of attention is the wonderful market square, with its cobbled surface and brightly decorated shop-windows. In the centre of the square there is an old water-pump. I suspect that today its function is more aesthetic than practical but it makes an interesting centre-piece nonetheless. The square also contains the Upper Wharfedale Museum where the visitor can find out more about the history and folk-lore of the surrounding area.

The village provides an excellent base for exploring Upper Wharfedale and there are a good selection of hotels and guest-houses for the visitor to choose from.

During the first three Saturdays in December Grassington hosts its own special Dickensian Festival. The streets are crammed full of stalls offering their festive wares, while the stallholders and many of the villagers dress themselves up in Dickensian-style costume to add a special flavour to the occasion.

There are no Mr. Bumbles about this morning as I make my way up through the village towards the open expanses of Grassington Moor.

Grassington Moor

The Dales Way climbs steadily upwards, first following a track and then to open moorland. I am now some appreciable height above the valley floor and the difference in terrain is very noticeable. The lush pastures of the riverside are replaced by coarse moorland grasses with occasional gorse bushes and the odd tree. Stretching ahead of me is a wild plateau with limestone bluffs off to my right. Down below to my left is the River Wharfe, currently hidden by the trees of the lower slopes.

The first part of Grassington Moor is known as Lea Green and it is a part of the ancient field settlement. Some accounts date this settlement as far back as the iron-age while others refer to it as Romano-Celtic.

Whatever the origins, that this area of ground was thought suitable for growing arable crops in days gone by leads to further questions because nobody would ever suggest that it would be suitable today. It is a fine sunny day today but it can easily be envisaged that the area would not be too pleasant in adverse conditions. The exposed and windswept hillside would certainly be no place for nurturing delicate crops. This would seemingly lead us to the conclusion that the climatic conditions of two thousand years ago were so much friendlier for agriculture than those of today. There are also reports that the Romans cultivated grapes as far north as York, so it would seem reasonable to assume that our ancestors enjoyed a much warmer climate than we do today.

Perhaps the current theory of global warming is only taking us back to normality following an intervening cold spell.

We will leave the meteorological aspects to one side, and take a look instead at one of the most noticeable geological features of Grassington Moor, the limestone pavements.

Limestone Pavements

Limestone pavements are to be found in various places around the world, and the Yorkshire Dales boasts some of the finest examples. The pavements here at Grassington Moor are not as pronounced as can be found at Malham Cove, but they are well worthy of mention.

The sediments that were later to form the original limestone of the area were deposited some 350 million years ago when plant and animal remains settled on the sea bed. Over time the sediments formed layers which were gradually compressed into strata's of rock. The formation of the layers caused "bedding planes" between each stratum. Eventually the action of the movements of the crust of the earth forced these sedimentary rocks towards the surface.

The next part of the formation was caused by the eroding effects of the ice ages. The ice-sheets wore away the covering and the force caused some of the rocks to shear along the bedding plane. When the glaciers finally retreated this left behind a flat table of limestone covered with scratches from the actions of the glaciers.

Limestone possesses a property of being very slightly soluble in water, and consequently the rains started to wear the tiny scratches into deeper grooves, and then eventually into sharp vertical crevasses in the rock. This process had the effect of turning the flat surface of the rock into the appearance of a pavement, with the slabs (known as clints), and the grooves (known as grykes) being the noticeable features. The whole process takes place over a period of many thousands of years.

The limestone does not even have to be exposed on the surface for the formation of pavements to occur. Water will still cut away at the limestone even if the rock is covered with soil. In fact the process is often faster underground than on the surface. The water will tend to be slightly acidic after dissolving some of the decomposed vegetation in the soil so making it a better solvent for the limestone. When the cuts and crevasses in the limestone become sufficiently large the soil will be easily washed away down the grykes leaving the limestone surface exposed.

Limestone pavements generally have an unusual ecology. Many of the areas where the pavements are to be found were formerly wooded, but were cleared for grazing animals. Grazing would normally wipe out many of the former woodland plant species, but those plants hidden in the grykes from the munching jaws of the animals would survive and thrive. As a consequence several woodland species still survive in areas of limestone pavement, although now isolated from their original habitat. An extraordinary example of the ability of life to survive despite the difficulties thrust at it.

Lime Kilns

With all of this limestone rock covering the moor it provided a plentiful source of building materials and there are several small quarries scattered across the hillside. Limestone also had other uses, one of them being the raw material for the production of "quicklime". This is principally powdered limestone with a high calcium content and is used for the making of mortars for buildings and in controlling the acidity of soils for agricultural purposes.

Here on Grassington Moor there is a lime kiln built into the rock. Kilns tended to be built where there was a plentiful supply of limestone and suitable fuel for the kiln in order to reduce the costs of transportation. This particular kiln is around 150 years old.

The process of manufacturing quicklime has been known since early times and is a fairly straightforward operation. The chemical equation for the calcification process is

$$CaCO_3 + heat = CaO + CO_2$$

When heated to 900 degrees Centigrade the partial pressure of carbon dioxide becomes equal to atmospheric pressure and the gas begins to dissipate into the air. By the time the temperature of the limestone reaches 1000 degree the partial pressure is nearly four times atmospheric pressure and the gas is fair flowing out of the rock. Increased temperatures however produce only "dead-burned" lime which is of very poor quality.

The limestone rock is first crushed into pieces of between one inch and two inches in size. This is the ideal size because the kiln fires must be able to breathe or else they will not properly burn. Larger pieces would not burn efficiently, while smaller pieces would simply suffocate the fire.

The kiln would be loaded in layers of crushed limestone and coal. The skill was to obtain the right balance of fuel and limestone to generate the correct temperature for the entire contents of the kiln. It can be easily appreciated that the hottest part will be at the centre above the air inlet with the contents cooling towards the outside. With the temperature being such a key element in the process it is no surprise to find that most kilns found around the country are of similar size because this has been proved to give the most efficient production.

A typical kiln would take one day to load, three days to burn, two more days to cool to a point where it could be handled and then a further day to unload. Therefore a kiln working flat-out could produce one batch of quicklime per week.

The powdered quicklime would then be transported to the local farms where it would be used to fertilise the acid soils.

I take a small detour to Conistone Pie to take in the view. The "Pie" is a limestone outcrop named after the small hamlet in the valley immediately below. It has the initial appearance of a tower, but as I approach closer I can clearly see the limestone cracks in the "walls". It makes for a truly marvelous viewing point for looking up and down the valley. After a short rest taking in the view I leave Conistone Pie behind and begin the gradual descent to the delightful village of Kettlewell.

Enclosure Acts and Drystone Walls

Walking towards Kettlewell I pass through an area of the valley that is criss-crossed by dry stone walls. It is the stereotype Yorkshire Dales scene. The walls are about four feet high and tend to run vertically straight up the hillside to the tree-line and are intersected at right-angles by similar walls following the contours of the valley. The end result is a chequered series of green pastures dotted with the white fleeces of sheep.

These walled pastures date from the late 1700's to early 1800's and were the result of the passing of various Enclosure Acts by Parliament.

As was all too often the case in those days, Acts of Parliament tended to be about the rights of the wealthy and privileged to deny access and rights to the general public, and the Enclosure Acts were no exception. Various Acts restricting access to land had been passed since the 12th century, but they became much more frequent during the years between 1750 and 1860. The idea behind the Enclosure Acts was to remove the rights of commoners to graze on open fields by "enclosing" them and taking them into private ownership. The fields in many areas of England were enclosed with fencing or hedges, but in the Yorkshire Dales the preferred method was to use dry stone walling.

Great tracts of land were rapidly swallowed up as walls were erected that extended high up the sides of the fells. The lands acquired by this measure become known as "intakes".

In some areas of the Yorkshire Dales the walls do not appear to be straight, but have an elongated "S" shape. Why did they build them like that, or is it just an optical illusion? The answer would appear to be that when the walls were first erected that they followed some of the old "ridge and furrow" patterns of the fields. The swing of the plough as it was turned at the end of the furrow would result in the edge of the field being curved. When the walls were constructed the builder simply followed these established lines.

The total area of land involved under the Enclosure Acts was quite staggering. The full passing of the Enclosure Acts required over 5,000 individual Acts of Parliament, and they resulted in the enclosure of over 21% of all of the land in England which amounted to almost 7 million acres.

Dry stone walling is a skill that is still very much in demand. Although it is much quicker to erect a wire fence in the first instance, by the time repairs and maintenance over a prolonged period of time are taken into consideration the dry stone wall starts to come into its own as an economic proposition. The walls can stand for many decades, and need little in the way of maintenance once they have been built.

Walls also provide additional benefits both to the farmer and the environment. Animals can readily obtain shelter from the elements and in poor weather sheep can often be found snuggled up against the stones as they seek refuge from the winds and rain. Mosses and wild flowers also find sheltered conditions among the stones in which they can flourish.

The construction of a dry stone wall will vary depending on local traditions. Here we will take a look at the basic double wall.

The new wall is started with two parallel rows of stones, and the builder carefully creates the wall so that the two rows of the wall effectively lean on to each other, each one supporting the other. At frequent intervals the builder will position a tie-stone or through-stone, laying it perpendicular to the other stones so that the two walls are tied together. These stones reinforce the wall and make it much stronger than a simple single wall.

To build a really strong wall with no large gaps showing between the stones requires great skill and experience. Selection of the right stone for each location is paramount and the skilled waller will take his time to choose each individual stone with care before placing it in its position.

The wall is generally finished with a row of cap stones. These stones are placed vertically with each one covering the full width of the wall. The additional weight of these stones provides additional downward force that helps to keep the wall below it bound together.

The stone walls provide a distinguishing feature of the Yorkshire Dales, and this area of Wharfedale just below Kettlewell has a particularly attractive abundance of them. My progress is inevitably slowed by the constant opening and shutting of the gates as I pass from field to field. Steadily I follow the way markers through the maze of fields and eventually I arrive at the track leading to the village of Kettlewell.

Kettlewell

Kettlewell is a very attractive village. It is well protected by the high surrounding fells and the additional shelter that this provides reputedly makes Kettlewell a warmer place to live than the other villages in Upper Wharfedale.

There are two explanations offered for the name of the settlement. Firstly that it is named after an Irish-Nordic chieftain by the name of Ketel, and the second that it is Anglo-Saxon in origin, deriving from the Saxon words Cetel Wella, meaning a gurgling stream. Take your pick from either of them.

In the olden days it would seem that Kettlewell functioned as a thriving market place, with merchants from Scotland and across the north of England being frequent visitors. During Norman times the ownership of the area was divided between the two monasteries of Coversham Abbey and Fountain Abbey. After the dissolution of the monasteries the estates were returned to the possession of the Crown. During the reign of Charles I by some obscure reasoning the village became allocated to be administered by the City Of London. Goodness knows how they came to work that one out, but inevitably this did not prove to be very successful way of running a settlement so far away and in 1656 the village and its surrounding area was purchased by a consortium of local yeomen.

The fortunes of Kettlewell as a market fell in the early 17th century, but in common with the villages situated lower down in Wharfedale prosperity returned in the early 19th century with the establishment of lead mining, cotton and weaving.

The footpath very conveniently brings me to the Kings Head Inn. This is a lovely old English pub with an inglenook fireplace and welcoming landlord. It dates from the 17th century and was first used as a mill and then later becoming the local workhouse. The Kings Head provides an excellent location for a well-deserved lunch before I set off along the River Wharfe for the rest of the day's walking.

Kettlewell is one of those relatively rare places where the road has been kept to one side of the village rather than the whole settlement being built around the thoroughfare. The road only just touches the village at one corner, so the village itself is very quiet with little traffic to disturb the peace and quiet.

The church looks to be old, but is in fact relatively new having only been consecrated as recently as 1885. An attractive lych gate stands at the entrance and is the setting for a quaint local tradition which enables the children of the village to gain some coins to spend in the local sweet-shop. When a wedding is held at the church the children of Kettlewell tie the gates together with brightly coloured ribbons and will only untie them to allow the groom to pass through to the churchyard after he has thrown them some coins.

Kettlewell still possesses a village stocks that stand by the side of the road. These are the low form of stocks, where the victim is seated on the ground with his (or her) ankles and arms held fast by the wooden boards. (The type where the villain is secured upright with neck and wrists secured is more correctly termed a pillory). I can't help but wonder if there is any relationship between the continued existence of the stocks and the complete absence of litter and graffiti in the locality.

If some of the streets look familiar it may be that the visitor is recognising the locations used in the making of a popular film. Kettlewell was used in 2002 for the location scenes for "Calendar Girls", the story of the Women's Institute members who stripped off for a charity calendar to raise money for Leukaemia Research.

The best time to visit Kettlewell would seem to be in August. This is when the village holds its annual Scarecrow Festival and there are literally hundreds of home-made scarecrows to be seen scattered around the countryside. It all began in 1994 with a "fun-day" to raise money for the local primary school, but it was so successful that it has since expanded into an annual fixture lasting several days.

There are no scarecrows to stare at today (or indeed any naked W.I. members), so I am off to cross the river at the bridge and to follow the Dales Way further up the Wharfe for the rest of the day.

Kettlewell to Buckden

The afternoon walk is going to cover a very different terrain to the one I experienced this morning. The wild moorland between Grassington and Kettlewell with its strenuous climbs and sharp slopes has been replaced by a quite distinct footpath and an almost imperceptible uphill walk alongside the meandering river. A later study of the map revealed rather surprisingly that for the four miles between Kettlewell and Buckden I climbed little more than 25metres. Needless to say this makes this part of the footpath very popular with the more casual walker, and I can see quite a few people dotted along the footpath ahead.

There is a reason for the more level ground in this part of the valley, which takes us back to the end of the last ice-age about 10,000 years ago. As the glaciers retreated this part of the valley would have once been a lake. The floor of the lake would have gradually been covered with sediment washed down from the upper reaches of the valley and resulted in the formation of a fairly flat lake-bed. Eventually a point would have been reached where the retreating glaciers would not have been able to provide sufficient water to keep the lake filled and so it would have gradually started to dry out. All that is left now is the infant River Wharfe meandering through a flat valley floor.

On my left are the remains of the spoil heaps from the New Providence Lead Mines. When the mines were in their former glory there were two water wheels here that powered a crushing plant and winding machine.

All along the sides of the valley there are quite a few stone barns dotted along the lower slopes. There must be a reason for them being here, but what could it be? When I found the answer it was no great surprise to me that it was another one of those sublime pieces of logic that were so obvious to our ancestors but that we do not tend to see straight away.

The fields where the barns stand were once hayfields. Farm workers would cut the hay and then store it in the loft of the barns. When winter came the cattle would be put in stalls within the barns. The feed was already available in the barns so that it was a fairly straightforward task to keep the feeding troughs replenished. Dung would be piled outside the barn ready for spreading on to the field to fertilise the next hay crop. This simple process of storing the feed where it grew and then building the cowsheds in the same place was clearly more efficient than transporting the hay to the farmyard.

Modern farming methods have resulted in the fields not being used for hay these days and the barns are no longer in regular use. Some are becoming derelict, although others are being maintained and preserved by the National Trust.

Large areas of Upper Wharfedale between Kettlewell and Beckermonds are managed by the National Trust. There is an excellent visitor centre in the Town Head Barn at Buckden detailing the work of the Trust and the flora and fauna of the locality.

The list of wildflowers is impressive and this spring the riverside meadows are awash with the different varieties. With the help of guidebooks I can identify some of the less-common species such as "Sweet Cicely" with its hint of aniseed scent, and the pink-spiked "Bistort". The summer months will bring out the vivid blue "Meadowsweet Cranesbill" and the fragrant "Meadowsweet". There are many more varieties to be found, and a family could spend an enjoyable day here just "spotting" wild flowers to see who can collect the most. Remember; please do not pick the wild flowers. Leave them for everyone to enjoy in their natural habitat.

Bird-watchers or "twitchers" as they are also known can also have a wonderful time in Upper Wharfedale. Dippers, Lapwings, Curlews and Wagtails are common, but I dearly want to see a Kingfisher. I have kept my eyes darting towards any trees and bushes along the riverbank that have looked as if they could be housing one of the distinctive blue birds, but to no avail. There are probably much too many people along the footpath today and the ever watchful and cautious King of the River is keeping well away.

It is very hard in these beautiful tranquil surroundings to remember that everything that I am seeing is not natural; it is man-made. Many people are rather taken aback by this revelation, but I can assure you that it is completely true. Almost all of the typical

English landscape that we enjoy so much is only like it is because that is the way that we have made it. If left to her own devices Mother Nature would have covered the valley floor with rich oak woodland. The valley sides would be covered with ash, elm and hawthorn while the hilltops would be capped with birch, hazel and wild scrub.

It took a long time but we managed to convert all of that into the Upper Wharfedale that we have today. The lower trees were cleared for settlements and farms. To expand the farms the hillsides and tops were slowly cleared to create summer pasture. Finally the slopes are kept clear by thousands of woolly-backed lawn mowers who munch through grass and seedlings as they wander over the landscape.

A wooden footbridge crosses the river to the hamlet of Starbotten. This unusual name appears to derive from Old English, derived from Staeurboten which translated as "the place where stakes are obtained". Starbotten is a pleasant little village with old houses and cottages lining its narrow streets. It is a popular turning point for walkers who take the path up the dale and return to Kettlewell. The presence of a nice pub for half-way refreshment, the "Hare and Hounds", does it no harm either.

Buckden

My steps continue alongside the river, and take me towards the charming village of Buckden. The name is simple; it means "the place where bucks are found". Herds of fallow deer were still freely roaming the area in the late 1940's but unfortunately it is rare to see even one now.

Buckden was originally founded by Percy, Duke of Northumberland as the main centre for the Longstrothe Hunting Forest. More correctly the area would have been known as The Longstrothedale Chase. The word "forest" was used in those days to define an area of wasteland or wilderness that was used for hunting and was owned by the King. If the hunting rights had been granted to a loyal subject then the area would be termed a "chase". All of the surrounding lands had been granted to the Percy family following the Norman Conquest.

During the Middle Ages the village would have been a very busy place, providing refreshment and entertainment for the hunting nobility and their entourages. Now there is only one inn, "The Buck Inn" remaining.

The River Wharfe has been steadily dwindling in size as I made my way up the dale, and above Buckden it reduces considerably. This is because one of its higher tributaries, the Buckden Gill, makes its significant contribution to the flows here. The beck collects its waters from the slopes of Buckden Pike that stands proudly behind the village at 2,300 feet high.

Up on the fell there is a memorial cross. Although I scan the hillside I am unable to find it, although I know it is up there somewhere. Back in 1942 a Wellington bomber carrying a crew of six Polish airmen crashed into Buckden Pike during a heavy blizzard. Only one member of the crew survived the crash. Bruised, cut, bleeding and with a shattered leg he dragged his broken body out of the wreckage and started to crawl away from the broken plane. After a few minutes he came across some new fox tracks in the snow. The airman reasoned that the only reason that a fox would be moving in this bad weather was to forage for food, which would only be available near to the farms. He made his mind up that his best chance for survival was to crawl along the tracks until he could find help. Driven by his ferocious will-to-live he dragged himself slowly downhill through the thickening snow. Eventually he was rewarded by reaching a farmhouse where he was taken in and transferred to hospital. To commemorate his comrades he later had the memorial cross erected on the hillside near to where the Wellington had crashed. In the foundations of the cross there is a bronze fox's head to commemorate the part that the airman believed that his vulpine saviour played in his survival.

There is something very tranquil about Buckden. A row of houses and the village shop stand back behind a village green. I am taking some photographs when I am accosted by one of the more elderly locals. "Beautiful isn't it?" he declares. Some people habitually ignore such interjections, and wondering why the "nutter" always picks on them, make mumbled excuses and shuffle off. I have often found that a polite response reveals something new and interesting. Today was going to be no exception. After I had enthusiastically agreed with his sentiments he went on to add "J.B.Priestley said this was the finest place in England". This took me by surprise and I found myself saying that I did not know Priestley came from here and before I knew what was happening I was receiving the full history.

J.B.Priestley

John Boynton Priestly was born on September 13th 1894 in Bradford, West Yorkshire. His father, Jonathan, was a schoolteacher and his mother, Emma, was a mill worker. John's mother passed away while he was still young and so he was mostly raised by his stepmother Amy.

During his childhood young John enjoyed a relatively prosperous lifestyle in cosmopolitan Edwardian Bradford. He would later write lovingly of the fond memories of his adolescent days.

The young Priestley was educated at Belle Vue School, but left at the age of sixteen to work in a wool agency. Although he had left school, Priestley harboured an ambition to be a successful writer, and penned many works on a voluntary basis to try and start a career. His first success was "Secrets of the Rag-Time King" that was published in 1912. He also wrote freelance contributions for newspapers and magazines.

When war broke out Priestley volunteered to join the Duke of Wellington's West Yorkshire Regiment and after initial training was sent to the front. Priestley survived the war, but was seriously wounded twice. Unlike many of his literary contemporaries he wrote little of his experiences at the time, only privately publishing a book of poetry "The Chapman of Rhymes" which he later tried to subdue by destroying copies.

After the war Priestley was awarded a small ex-officers grant which he used to go and study at Trinity Hall, Cambridge. Upon leaving university Priestley moved to London, married his childhood sweetheart Pat Tempest with whom he had two daughters, and set about creating a dynamic career as a writer. Sadness entered his life with the death of his wife through illness. He found happiness again and married Jane Wyndham-Lewis in 1926 and together they produced two daughters and a son.

Priestley worked prodigiously at his writing, and started to move away from fiction producing his first major work of non-fiction "The Good Companions". He also started to turn towards the challenges of writing for the theatre, and in 1932 published his first play "Dangerous Corner".

Just as it seemed that a promising career as a theatre writer was beckoning, Priestley set out on a new venture. He had been invited to join a project titled "English Journey" where the intention was that he would write about the way of life of the people in the industrial areas. However, the journey he made and the people he discovered made such an influence on Priestley that the project was transformed into a full social commentary on the English social structure. Priestley's contributions resulted in him becoming firmly established as a leading figure in the field of social studies. His acute awareness and depth of understanding that he was able to communicate to the wider world was to have a great influence on the rest of his life.

During the Second World War Priestly turned his talents to radio. He became a broadcaster with the BBC and developed a key role for himself. The BBC had an important task in those days to help the war effort by keeping up the general morale of the British people. Priestley soon became very popular for his speciality "Postscripts" that were broadcast after the early evening news. The programme was intended to feature vivid descriptions of all of the good things in life that Britain would enjoy after the war but Priestley's social conscience started to influence the scripts in a different direction. He introduced some of the social aspects that he had discovered while working on "English Journey" and started to use some of the air-time to press for welfare reform. This angered many people on the political right, but found a resonance with the majority of the population.

Priestley was a man of formidable energies and when the war was over he became involved with many different and wide-ranging projects. Straight after the cessation of hostilities he made an attempt to enter the political arena by standing as an Independent candidate in the 1945 General Election. In hindsight it was probably a blessing in disguise for him that he was not elected, for it would have been difficult for him to pursue such a diverse range of interests as well as keep up such a prodigious output of writings if he had been hampered by the additional demands of a career at Westminster.

During the 1950's Priestley travelled the country vigorously campaigning against nuclear armament. As part of his energetic campaign he composed an essay for "New Statesman" magazine entitled "Britain and the Nuclear Bombs". The journal received so many letters after the article was published that the momentum carried forward into a life of its own. All of this high-profile activity generated much interest and brought many like-minded people together. The end result was the formation of the Campaign for Nuclear Disarmament. Priestley was rewarded for his efforts by being appointed to the office of Vice President.

It was no great surprise that Priestley's reputation quickly spread and he became in huge demand to make contributions to the work of many distinguished bodies. Priestley accepted a position as a delegate to UNESCO in New York. It proved to be a greater life-changing experience than he first thought because it was there that he first became acquainted with archaeologist and poet Jaquetta Hawkes. Jaquetta was later to become Priestley's third wife following his divorce from Jane. With Jaquetta he spent some time touring around the United States which provided the inspiration for his book "Journey Down a Rainbow". The couple later made their made their home in Stratford-upon-Avon.

When he returned to England Priestley became heavily involved in the foundation of the Arts Council and worked tirelessly for the benefit of the arts in general.

Priestley continued to be a prodigious writer and his work was published until well into the 1970's. As is often the case with great men, formal public recognition did not come to him until his later years. He was proposed for both a knighthood and a peerage but turned them both down. In 1977 he accepted the award of the Order of Merit.

Priestley never actually lived in Upper Wharfedale, but loved the scenery here and would visit the area on many occasions throughout his life. He died on August 14th 1984 just a month before he would have reached the magic hundred. It was his wish for his ashes to be buried at the pretty church at Hubberholme, which is my next port of call.

Hubberholme

For reasons best known to the people who decide upon these sorts of things, the highest section of the Wharfe valley that stretches above Buckden to the watershed at Cam Fell is known as Langstrothedale and not Wharfedale. So to be absolutely correct my journey through the delights of Upper Wharfedale has ended and I am entering new territory.

The tiny village of Hubberholme is situated only about a mile and a half upstream from Buckden but by the time I reach Hubberholme Bridge both the river and the road have narrowed considerably. This instills in me the feeling that I am gradually entering a lonelier and wilder place, becoming ever more isolated and remote with every step I take.

Hubberholme was identified in the Domesday Book as "Huburgham", and was recorded at that time as being a part of the manor of Kettlewell. It consists of a tiny scattering of houses and farms, and prompts the pedantic question of whether to call it a village or a hamlet. What is the difference between a village and a hamlet? The answer is fairly simple because as everyone should know the difference is that one has a church, whilst the other is a play by William Shakespeare. The church is tucked around the corner, but alongside the bridge is a long, white, slate-roofed building which can boast a unique piece of trivia.

The George Inn is situated adjacent to the bridge on what could loosely be termed the "main road" of the village. Every New Year's Day the inn is the venue for the unusual tradition of the annual land-letting auction that goes by the grand-sounding name of the "Hubberholme Parliament".

Since the early 18th century it has been the custom for local plots of poor quality land to be let by auction for the ensuing year. Anyone could bid for the rights to use the plots, but there were some strict local rules that had to be followed. The prospective buyers, sellers and administrative clerks to record the transactions would meet in "The George" on the day of the Parliament. Using such a public place ensured that there would be plenty of witnesses to the proceedings. The auctioneer or chairman would light a candle and the bidding for the various lots would begin. The prospective buyers would declare their bids, probably exclaiming that they were overpaying and that the landowners were robbing them blind. The sellers and land agents no doubt also did their very best to talk up the value of the land with all sorts of dubious benefits. All the fun of the free-market!

Sellers and bidders would exchange their offers while the candle burned, and as the flame burned down the wax the activity would increase and the auction become more urgent. When the candle finally extinguished that was the end of the proceedings. The last bid recorded before the final flicker died away would be the price that would have to be paid. The deal was done and dusted for the duration of the year.

Having been involved in several attempts to buy properties through all of the jungle of complexities and uncertainties of the modern "buying chain" this method would appear to have a lot of potential benefits. I wonder if I could persuade my local estate agents to adopt the custom.

The second building of note in Hubberholme is the church that I mentioned a little earlier. St Michael and All Angels is sited by the river among a light screening of fir trees. There has been a church on this site since at least the 13th century when it was known as St.Oswald of Huberham and was maintained by the monks of Coverham Abbey.

Inside the church the pews are constructed of beautifully hand-carved oak, and bear the distinctive "mouse" trademark of craftsman Robert Thompson who was known as "The Mouse Man of Kilburn"

A further notable feature of this church is its unusual oak rood loft which is one of very few examples of this once common architectural feature remaining in England. The reason that almost all similar structures disappeared is because Queen Elizabeth I threw one of her hissy-fits and issued an edict in 1558 that all such decorative features on churches should be destroyed. That the loft remains is proof that either the finer details of royal decrees failed to reach this outpost of the realm, or the good citizens of the parish of Hubberholme decided that it was their church and if "yon madam down south wants t' pull down our rood she would have t' come up and pull t' bugger down 'erself". I will leave you to decide, but I do hope that it was local rebellious forces that were responsible for preserving their heritage.

Sheep Farming

The bulk of the population on these hills are sheep, so this would be a good opportunity to take a look at one of Britain's oldest industries, and one where believe it or not we are still among the world leaders.

There are approximately 40 million sheep in this country, and that is a lot of sheep. The value of sheep production to the economy was calculated at £822 million. Typically the average visitor could come across as many as 40 different breeds, but including the special rare breeds there are many more. The National Sheep Association has pictures of 85 separate breeds on its website, starting with Badger Faced Welsh Mountain going through the alphabet and finally arriving at the strange sounding Zwartbles sheep.

Sheep farming has been part of the British countryside for more than 6,000 years. During that period the husbandry and cross-breeding has resulted in the evolution of specialist breeds ideally suited to their specific environments. The sheep were also bred to give higher yields of the two major products of sheep farming; meat and wool.

In times gone by Britain was renowned for its wool and many fortunes were made in the industry. Many of our great churches particularly those of Gloucestershire and Suffolk were financed from the production and merchandising of wool. In the House of Lords the Lord Chancellor still sits on the "woolsack" to signify his authority.

When sheep farming was in its infancy all those many years ago the natural inclination of the animals was to moult. The farmers would then gather the wool together and use that to make yarn. Selective breeding resulted in the wool staying on the sheep and needing to be shorn off in the fleeces that we are familiar with today. British sheep today have been bred to produce three different types of wool; carpet wool, down wool and long wool. Each has its own characteristics making it more suitable for certain applications.

Shearing takes place either in early summer or just before the sheep are housed for the winter. The process is necessary to prevent the sheep from overheating under the summer sun or within the confines of indoor winter quarters. Most of the shearing is carried out by teams of skilled professional shearers, usually from Australia or New Zealand, who can strip fleeces from a sheep faster than a barber can do a short-back-and-sides. And they probably don't ask the sheep where they are going on holiday and if they would they like "something for the weekend".

In the Middle Ages wool was England's most important export. The product was highly sought after throughout Europe and fortunes were made. These days it is somewhat different. The UK is still the world's 7th largest producer of wool, but the high value is no longer there. The development of modern fibres and textiles has displaced the requirement for traditional wool. Over 60,000 tonnes of wool were gathered last year, but at an average price of less than 50p per kilogram the farmers are able to achieve little more than cover the cost of shearing.

It is lamb for meat that provides the farmer with his income today. Each lamb will provide for between 16 to 18Kg (35lbs to 40lbs) of meat. This will be put into a wide variety of dishes, from the top quality lamb joints and my own favourite, "Lamb Henry" all the way through to shepherds pie and offal dishes such as the haggis.

Let us take a look at a typical year on a sheep farm. Each farmer will have their own preferred dates for maximum efficiency which will depend very much on the local climate. Hilltop farms in Scotland will be very much later than lowland pastures in the south of England, and the farms in the Yorkshire Dales will tend to be somewhere in the middle. The breeding ewes will undergo "flushing" in August/September. This is where the ewe will be fed an enriched diet to prepare her for breeding. Then in October/November she will be put to the ram. A typical flock will be divided up so that there are about 40 ewes for every ram.

Now, who knows why sheep have coloured splodges on their backs? This results from a simple yet very efficient monitoring method. The ram is fitted underneath with a device known as a "raddle". This is a strap carrying a pad coated with a very indelible dye. It is terrible stuff and just will not come off anything it comes into contact with leaving behind a considerable stain. So when the ram has covered a ewe she will have the tell-tale marking on her, and the shepherd will be able to separate the impregnated ewes from the others, so ensuring that the entire flock is covered and not just the more enthusiastic and frisky ones.

The lambing season is March/April. Again this will be determined by the suitability of the local climate. The lambing process is quite quick. The ewe will generally wander off to be on her own, and the first lamb will appear about an hour later, followed by a second within about 15 minutes. Some breeds, usually specially bred for harsh hilly conditions will only generally produce one lamb. After only a period of 20 minutes or so the lambs will be looking for their first feed.

After three days the lambs have their tails "docked" by having the tail "ringed" to cut off the blood flow. This action drastically reduces the possibilities of fly strike which can cause severe bacterial infection in flocks if it is allowed to become established. Whilst all lambs will have their tails ringed, for the young males there is a further hazard that awaits them at the same time. The lucky ones will be selected to join the breeding stock and have a life of frolicking around fitted with their own personal raddle. The unfortunate will be castrated and sentenced to an autumn or winter trip to the abattoir. These lambs are known as "wethers" and will be able to be mixed with the ewes and female lambs because having undergone their debilitating process they will have lost much of their natural aggression.

Weaning occurs during the months of May and June with the lambs rapidly gaining in weight, some as much as 0.5kg every day. During this time the lambs will be earmarked with their flock reference and individual identification number.

In August and September the first lambs destined for market will be moved to the richer grass pastures to fatten up before being sent for slaughter. The majority of the lambs will be fattened up during the period from October to January and then follow their former flock-mates to the slaughter house.

The sheep farmer has to go through all these stages whilst making sure that his flock stays free from infection that could have severe consequences for his livelihood. It looks like a leisurely lifestyle today, with lambs gamboling around with their mothers in a typically English country scene. I can only imagine how hard it must be to look after the same flocks in winter when the winds howl, the snow covers the ground and the only way to feed the flock is to try and get the Land Rover up the hillside.

That is sheep farming, and after considering everything that happens on the farm the price of a couple of lamb chops does not seem anywhere near as expensive as it did a while ago.

Hubberholme to Beckermonds

There are some woodlands on the slopes to my right, but the feeling of isolation increases as I continue up the valley. The footpath keeps close to the river after leaving Hubberholme. I can see that the river is noticeably shallower now, being only a few inches deep in places. The road on the opposite bank rises and falls along the side of the dale like a mini roller-coaster. A small procession of around a dozen old cars is making its way along it, obviously out for some kind of "club run" in the countryside. The owners must have confidence in the mechanical soundness of their prized possessions if they have brought them out to these remote parts. There are good reasons that many of the local inhabitants all tend to drive 4x4's and it is not to impress the other mums at the school gate like their city counterparts. I too would feel much more secure driving a Land Rover than an old "Ford Popular".

It is getting into the late afternoon and it is a fine day for walking with the sun out and a gentle cooling breeze. These are ideal conditions for getting a few extra miles under my belt. I have changed my original plan which was to end my day at

Hubberholme. The weather forecast for tomorrow is horrible and I want to get some of the distance covered today while the going is good.

Yockenthwaite Farm is quickly reached. It is an odd-sounding name, but has a very logical origin. In 1241 the site was recorded as Yoghannes Thweit so giving a definite pointer to its origin. The first part of the name relates to the old Irish name of Eogan, and thwaite is a fairly common name suffix meaning clearing. So Yockenthwaite is simply a handed-down version of Eogan's Clearing, which remembering that this area used to be covered with forest is a perfectly logical name.

Yockenthwaite Farm has been in the same family since 1842 and is noted for the high quality of its lamb. The non-intensive way in which the young lambs are reared results in a higher quality of meat for the table. If you are interested in sampling this quality fayre packs of meat can be purchased direct from the farmhouse or via the internet.

The path continues across the field from the farm but I can see that there is a very attractive single-track stone bridge leading to the farm from the road. I take a small diversion down to the river in order to take a few photographs, the afternoon light being just perfect to bring out the tones of the stonework.

The bridge is an old packhorse bridge, and although it sees little use today it was once part of a busy thoroughfare for supplies from Settle to Hawes. For most general supplies packhorse trains were the main means for moving goods around the country. The owners, or drivers, were the Eddie Stobarts of earlier times. A train could consist of forty or more horses and ponies, with only a driver plus one or two assistants to guide and look after them on their journey. Each animal would have panniers slung over their backs with baskets or sacks hanging on either side. To keep the horse balanced the weight had to be evenly spread, but even so an individual animal would typically transport up to two hundredweight of goods at a time.

Back on the way-marked path I soon pass a lime kiln, and then come across a circle of stones. This particular group is known as "Giants Grave" and consists of a ring of about 30 stones in a perfect circle. "Giants Grave" dates from the early Bronze Age and is believed to once have had a larger ring of stones around it. As is usually the case with such features nobody really knows why the stones were placed here in the first place. The normal assumption that is made is that it possesses some kind of religious significance.

The next farm up the dale is Deepdale, and the path crosses the river at Deepdale Bridge. The river is very different now. It still retains a reasonable width, but the shallow waters now race over smooth stones that have been polished over thousands of years of attrition. Small cascades add little white flecks to the surface and the rays of the sun induce sparkles that catch the eye.

I am now becoming even more remote. The road is no more than a single track and the path I am on is probably nearly as wide. There are few trees now, just the occasional bush. There are still plenty of birds around, and everywhere there are sheep, but people are now scarce. In fact I have not seen anybody else since passing through Deepdale.

I arrive at Beckermonds which is just a handful of houses nestling into a hollow by the stream. Beckermonds is a simple place name that originates this time from Danish, Beckur meaning stream and Munds for mouth. Two streams meet here, the Oughtershaw Beck and the Green Field Beck and the waters have a lively tussle with each other at the confluence point.

I have been informed that if I am lucky that I may be able to see a pair of Peregrine Falcons who are reported to have made their nest here, but on this fine late afternoon they prove to be elusive.

Effectively this is the end of my walk up Wharfedale. Tomorrow I will return to this point and set off to follow up the Oughtershaw Beck and then cut across the watershed of the Pennines at Cam Houses to drop down the other side to the quaint picturesque village of Dent.

It has been a glorious day and I am making terrific progress. However, as they say in all the hill-walking guidebooks, weather conditions can change suddenly.

DAY THREE

OUGHTERSHAW TO GEARSTONES

8 MILES

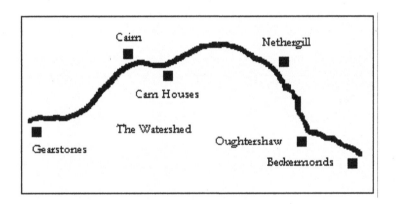

Oughtershaw

It is raining.

Actually I am doing the Yorkshire weather an injustice. It is absolutely pelting down and to make matters worse the wind is getting up as well. The clouds are very low. Not that I can really make out any individual clouds because the sky is just a dark grey canopy interspersed with bits of even darker grey.

I attempt to cheer myself up by pointing out to my darling wife that it is not too bad because I am still dry. I get a wry smile back. Then she goes and spoils my morale-boosting illusions by reminding me that I was still in the car and that I needed to get out and start walking.

I wave goodbye and arrange that we will meet in the late afternoon at the village of Dent. There is a craft market in Hawes that will be occupying the "Dearly Beloved" for most of the day. I just hope that she remembers that Hawes is the home of the Wensleydale Creamery and buys some for tonight's supper. "It's a cracking cheese Gromitt!"

Beckermonds looks very different this morning. Yesterday it was quite the idyllic little place with lovely farmhouses glowing in the sunshine and a lively stream trickling happily over the stones. Overnight this idyll had been transformed into a grim and desolate landscape with its houses looking dull and austere against the grey background of a leaden sky. The lively stream was still here, but today there was a new stream rushing through the village and it was pouring down the narrow lane leading to up to Oughtershaw. Can you guess which way my route was going?

I splashed my way up the hill, which turned out to be much longer and steeper than it first looked. The exertions made me quite breathless and I was relieved to reach the relatively level terrain of the village itself.

Oughtershaw is the last real settlement in Wharfedale, everything higher up being just farmsteads. Shaw is an Old English word referring to a wooded area providing shelter, so Oughtershaw is the outer area offering shelter. This would appear to refer to the settlement being on the edge of the Longstrothe Forest so providing the last shelter before the traveler encountered the exposed higher moorland.

The village provides just a few houses and Oughtershaw Hall, a relatively new building being a mere 150 years or so old. There is also a fine small chapel that would make an excellent photograph if it were not for the miserable conditions. A little further along the lane I discover a Celtic cross and I am somewhat puzzled as to what it is doing here. My later researches reveal that the cross is not a legacy of some early Celtic settlement, but a memorial placed there by the villagers of Oughtershaw to commemorate the Silver Jubilee of the reign of Queen Victoria in 1887.

The road ahead leads onwards to Hawes, but my route turns off here along a wide track. My direction from this point will be heading due west; straight into the wind that uncomfortably appears to be growing in strength.

Over The Watershed to Cam Houses

I must admit that it could be a lot worse. The best part of two hundred quid's worth of Berghaus coat is doing a grand job of keeping the rain out, although I have to keep my head bowed to avoid getting a face full of rain. As the wise man once said "There is no such thing as bad weather, only inadequate clothing. I cheerfully congratulate myself on my wise selection of outerwear and set off along the track.

The guidebook describes the farmstead of Nethergill as "austere" and today I can easily see why. Yesterday I could entertain thoughts that it must be lovely to live in such a remote area, but today the true hardships of such an existence become all too apparent. Following the track at least allows me to keep going at a reasonable pace. Below me the flat floor of the watershed is covered with small pools and channels that make up the headwaters of the River Wharfe. It would be a real struggle trying to cross the Pennines by that route, so I am grateful for the relative ease that this track provides. It seems that I am soon at Swarthgill but appearances can be deceptive. A glance at my watch reveals that it has taken far longer than I had planned because the headwind must have considerably slowed my progress.

Ahead of me I can just about make out the vague outlines of the buildings of Cam Houses. They appear to be a lot further away than they are indicated to be on the map. This is probably because the visibility is becoming very poor and playing tricks with my mind.

It is not only the visibility that is getting poor. There has been a rapid deterioration in the conditions underfoot. The track has come to an end and the path is now crossing over open land that has become decidedly soggy. Progress is becoming painfully slow as I squelch and slide through the boggy terrain. Each time I turn my head it results in another windswept spray of water finding its way into the confines of my coat hood. My walking trousers have now given up on any pretence of conforming to their claim of "water resistant" that is printed on to the label stitched into their rear. They have become sodden and cling to my legs so increasing my discomfort.

Somewhere on the ground in the saddle below is the actual watershed. A magical point where the Oughtershaw Beck runs eastwards to form the River Wharfe and the Cam Beck departs in the opposite direction to eventually become the River Ribble. With the amount of rain now falling on the watershed it is very probable that the two waters have joined up by now and somewhere down there is a puddle that is feeding both water systems simultaneously from its opposite ends.

A derelict barn provides some welcome respite from the elements for a few minutes. The shelter gives me some time to hunt through the rucksack for the "Snickers" bar that will give me some much needed nourishment.

Thus fortified I trudge onwards and ascend a final slope to the farmstead of Cam Houses. On a brighter day I would have been greeted with fine views across the watershed and down each side of the valleys but today it is not to be. Cam Houses has been in existence as a group of farms for centuries, and I can not help but wonder why people through the ages have chosen to eke out their existence in such a lonely spot. Even as these thoughts are passing through my mind I am aware of the Yin and Yan of those thoughts. If I was here yesterday in the bright sunshine and still air I would no doubt have been envious of the people who are able to live in splendid isolation up here on the moors with all of this wonderful scenery just outside their doors.

Over the Top and the High Road to Gearstones

Immediately after Cam Houses the Dales Way provides me with some unexpected sanctuary in the form of the Cam Woodlands. A path has been cut through the trees and today this woodland provides a welcome relief from the continual soaking I have been receiving. The guidebook describes this part of the walk as a "brief and gloomy interlude", but today it is a glorious haven of dryness.

All good things must come to an end and I emerge on the upper side of the woods to be confronted by a slope rising steeply into the mists. Somewhere up there is the literal "high point" of my day, indeed the literal "high point" of the whole walk. A cairn of stones marks the spot where the Dales Way attains its highest altitude at 1705 feet (520m). I set off this morning from Beckermonds that is at a height of around 1000 feet so I have climbed a fair way up today.

I reach the cairn and find a marker informing me that this is also where the Dales Way intersects with the Pennine Way. The two long-distance trails will travel together for the next mile or so before proceeding on their separate ways. I have also reached the "Cam High Road", a track allegedly dating back to prehistoric times. The track is very straight and was utilised by the Roman General Julius Agricola in his campaigns against the Brigantes in the 1st century. Whatever benefits the track gave to the Roman Legions could not have been as welcome as the benefits it was giving me now. After spending what seemed like an eternity (but was really only an hour or so) bog-trotting through difficult terrain the relatively easy walking facilitated by this track was an absolute god-send.

Sometimes in life magical things happen. Just when it seems that everything was against me today, nobody loved me anymore and why on earth have I bothered to flog myself through wind, rain and mud to reach this exposed ridge everything suddenly changes.

The rain stops, the wind drops and the skies start to brighten. It has happened often to me before but it is still an odd sensation when the weather suddenly improves. The drumming of the rain lashing down on my hood had been an almost continuous racket since setting off this morning, and now it was strangely quiet. The pleasure of throwing back the hood and exposing my head again was wildly liberating.

All of the guidebooks eulogize about the dramatic vistas of Penyghent, Ingleborough and Whernside from this track. When I set off this morning I thought that I was going to miss out on these sights but the Gods have decided to smile on me today. After all of the morning struggles against the elements I am rewarded by a glorious walk along the track during the early afternoon. As the skies continued to clear more of the surrounding hills are teasingly revealed to my view. It was easy walking, taking a steady downhill route and allowing me to absorb the scenery. With the weather being the way that it has been I am not surprised to be completely alone on the track and I can enjoy myself in splendid isolation.

The peak of Ingleborough lays directly ahead, Whernside, which has the honour of being Yorkshires highest point is sited at 2 o'clock and Pen-y-ghent lies to the south at about 10 o'clock. It is interesting to consider the names of these three mountains because, although they are geographically close together, their titles have different derivations. Whernside is derived from Old Norse, whern meaning millstone and saettr meaning summer pasture. Ingleborough takes its origins from Old English where it means "fort on the hill". However it is Pen-y-ghent that is the most interesting. Many people when asked where Pen-y-ghent is will usually answer "Wales" unless they know otherwise. Who can blame them because "Pen" is indeed the Welsh word for hill. In welsh Pen-y-ghent translates as the "hill of the border". In ancient times the Welsh language was spoken much more widely than it is today and the name of this hill possibly signifies that this was considered a limit of the welsh speakers.

The three hills form the challenging "Three Peaks" walk, and standing here looking at the tops (and the drops between them) it appears a daunting task indeed. The walk connecting the three peaks covers a little over 25 miles and involves a total climb of 5,287 feet (1,627m). One for me to mark down for the future. For now I must content myself that the mists have lifted to reveal these magnificent views. Any reader who wants to find out more about the "Three Peaks" can do no better than refer to Mike Brockhurst's excellent website at www.walkingenglishman.com

I am well behind my time schedule and it is going to be much later than anticipated before I eventually reach the sanctuary of Dent. Is it worth pressing on today, or do I cut my day short at the end of the track? If I stop short of my plan will I be able to catch up tomorrow or the next day? Fortunately I have allowed an extra day for contingency and so decide to put it to good use. I will stop early today and reschedule the rest of the walk to cover three days instead of two.

I punch the numbers in to the keypad and hope that for once my good lady has left her phone switched on. (Why do people have mobiles and then never switch them on?). Fortunately I was in luck twice, first by obtaining a strong enough signal to connect and then secondly by hearing her answering voice. Yes it was fun at the craft fair, and yes she was nearly finished and would shortly leave after getting "a couple of other things" (which loosely translates as "I can just manage to fill another bag with goodies first"), and then meet me at the spot marked "Gearstones" on the map that looks to be only a short walk from where the track I am currently wandering along meets with the main road.

Half an hour later the track crosses a footbridge over the infant River Ribble just before reaching the road. From the footbridge I could see the familiar blue Ford Focus pass along the road in the distance, coming to a halt a little way along.

"A bit wet are we?" was the jovial greeting. This was quickly followed by a more stern "Don't bring those wet things in the car". This is why anyone passing by at that precise time would have seen a middle-aged man throw a pair of boots, a coat and pair of very soggy trousers into the boot of a car before leaping bare-legged in to the passenger seat

"It will be better tomorrow", I confidently announced. "It can't be as wet as this again".

Idiot.

DAY FOUR

HOLME HILL TO LINCOLNS INN BRIDGE

17.5 MILES

Dentdale

N o prizes for guessing the weather today.

It was as if the intervening hours had never happened.

The only difference as I stood at the gateway to Gearstones was that I was wearing (for the meantime) dry clothes. Everything else was the same misty rainy soggy misery that I started out in yesterday.

I have decided to take a slight diversion from the official path this morning to try and make good time and attempt to compensate for the shortened day yesterday. The Dales Way official route would start by going up part of Holme Hill and then contouring around Gayle Moor. The first stage of this route is reported to be a good path, but then the waymarked path crosses an area known as Stoops Moss which is described in the guide-book as wet and boggy at the best of times. Today it would probably just be a morass of sludge and ooze that would try to suck my boots off. This would be an extremely morale-sapping struggle being so close to the start of the day. Therefore I am going to make an adjustment to my plan and follow the road down through Dentdale until I reach Cowgill and then rejoin the official Dales Way at that point and proceed to Dent.

The walk along the B6255 towards the junction to Dent takes me virtually due north. The wind and rain are more westerly today so at least the rain is not straight in my face today. The road itself is relatively straight and flat with only moderate rises and falls. However I am still at an altitude of just over a thousand feet and the road is very exposed. There is something about being in these wild isolated areas, and in their own special way the mists add to the beauty rather than detract from it. On either side the moorland stretches out but eventually blends into mist with the peaks that highlighted my afternoon yesterday hiding behind the curtain of cloud. To my right (east) lays the expanse of Gayle Moor and the watershed area of Cam House while on my left is Blea Moor, with the heights of Whernside obscured by the adverse conditions. Behind me stand Ingleborough and Pen-y-ghent, both invisible in their cloudy shrouds.

I reach the road junction and turn left towards Dent. Straight into the wind and rain. The first mile is along the exposed northern edge of Blea Moor and is a gradual uphill section. Eventually I reach the top of the pass and before me is the steady downhill route to Dent, and through the mists I can make out the outline of the Dent Head Viaduct.

After only a short period I pass the signs signifying that I am leaving Yorkshire and entering the county of Cumbria. Not that in these isolated places are there any noticeable differences that can be detected between the two administrations. My immediate thoughts are that it is raining just as hard in both counties!

It was not too long into my walk down the dale when I was richly rewarded for my choice of route. Scurrying about under the cover of a roadside tree I spied a red squirrel. Mr. Nutkins hastily scrambled up the tree to rest himself on a branch and cautiously stare at me while I entered into a mad flurry to claw my camera out of the rucksack and fit the telephoto lens. Unfortunately I was much too slow and the squirrel raced off to continue his business elsewhere. Still, it was an unexpected bonus for the start of the day.

Settle to Carlisle Railway

I pass under the Dent Head Viaduct that carries the celebrated Settle-Carlisle railway line. It is an impressive viaduct, but then again the entire Settle to Carlisle Railway is a very impressive piece of civil engineering. The railway is undoubtedly the most scenic stretch of track in Britain and to travel along its length is a very popular activity for both tourists and railway enthusiasts.

The necessity for the initial construction of the line was totally illogical and resulted from a typical piece of business bloody-mindedness during the late 1860's. At that time there were already good railway links to Scotland that utilised the obvious low-level east coast and west coast routes. The problem for the rapidly expanding Midland Railway Company was that the other railway companies would not grant them any access to these lines. Midland Railway Company was determined that such setbacks were not going to halt their progress and took the bold decision that they would link the Midlands to Scotland with their own railway line. They would create this new link by taking the most direct route possible, by blasting their way straight up the through the Pennines, the backbone of England. It will only take the briefest of glimpses at a map to show how ambitious this project was. To maintain a reasonably level line would require the building of a series of very high viaducts and dynamiting several tunnels through the mountains. Totally undaunted by the size of the task that is exactly what they did.

It took six years of hard work before the railway was opened on May 1st 1876. There were no mechanical diggers in those days, and all of the work was carried out by "navvies" using picks, shovels and the occasional stick of dynamite. Thousands of workers were required just for this section of the railway. Ramshackle shanty-towns were set up near to the three big viaduct sites at Ribblehead, Dent Head and Arten Gill in order to accommodate the incoming labourers. Such was the demand for lodgings that all through Dentdale the houses and farms were crammed full with itinerant workers. Blacksmiths, stonemasons and a whole host of other support trades set up their workshops in the area. Hard manual labour is thirsty work and there was a proliferation of temporary ale-houses to slake the thirst of the dry-throated navies. For a short-time this must have been the dales equivalent to the Klondike.

The structure that I am passing under is just one of seventeen impressive viaducts that can be found along the 72 miles of this remarkable railway. The most famous is the much photographed 24-arched Ribblehead Viaduct that is situated a few miles south of where I am now. Before being able to reach the viaduct towering above me the track has already passed over Ribblehead and then plunged beneath Blea Moor through the longest tunnel on the railway. No sooner has it emerged from that blackness than it finds itself here crossing Dent Head. The railway continues in a similar style all the way to Carlisle. It is 72 miles of outstanding civil engineering. The views from the carriages are incredible and it is well worth making the effort to experience this wonderful railway journey.

Dent Marble

The magnificent Victorian structure of Dent Head Viaduct seems to be out of all proportion to the small stream that it crosses. This little trickle is the very infant stage of the River Dee. I will be more-or-less following this stream from this point until its confluence with the River Lune later in the day.

It is an attractive walk down the road towards Dent. Once under the viaduct the sides of the valley afford more protection from the winds, and more trees along the roadside give some additional shelter. The water level in the river has swollen up with the recent downpours giving the river an extra vitality. Small limestone ledges across the riverbed form small waterfalls that link together to provide lively cascades. Mostly the river runs tight to the side of the road, and there is a succession of small stone bridges that lead to the various dwellings that are tucked into the sides of the valley.

Stonehouse was formerly a stone works owned by Richard Alderson that was much prized for producing black Dent Marble. The local stone is peculiar to this small area with the majority of the stone being found in the valley of Arten Gill that cuts its way down the nearby hillside. This much sought-after material was a form of high-carbon black limestone with an unusually high fossil content. When it was highly polished the stone gave the effect of a glossy black foundation embedded with a very appealing white marbling. Dent Marble became extremely popular during the mid-nineteenth century for the manufacture of fireplaces and interior columns. The largest fireplace was made in 1843 for the Winter Palace of the Tsar of Russia in St. Petersburgh. I will see a smaller but no less elegant example on display at the Dent Village Heritage Centre later this morning.

The demand for Dent Marble was relatively short-lived. Cheaper Italian marble began to flood the market, and gradually the Stonehouse works were forced to close. The unpolished stone can still be seen in Arten Gill, and there are reputedly many examples of Dent Marble fireplaces still in regular use in the local farms and houses.

Dent Brewery

There is a more modern business a little lower down the valley and I am sorely tempted to take a small diversion to see if there are any free samples going. If I said that their award-winning products included "Golden Fleece", Ramsbottom", "Rambrau" and "T'owd Tup" you may at first think that there is a certain "sheepiness" incorporated into their range. The sheep theme continues all through their product range but there is nothing "sheepish" about their products which are full-blooded, strong-flavoured and highly recommended real ales. Hollins, near Cowghill, is the home of the Dent Brewery which is one of the most isolated breweries in Britain. Isolated it may be, but it is a fully modernized top-of-the-range "microbrewery" run by local brewer Paul Goodyer. Using spring water from Rise Hill and carefully selected malts and hops the brewery has won so many CAMRA awards that it is difficult to keep count of them all. Some of the brews are also available in bottles so you may find some at your local discerning "Off Licence".

Dent Brewery's biggest seller is surprisingly not sheep related in its name, but called "Aviator". It is an amber-coloured ale with a strong hoppy flavour, just a hint of citrus and an alcohol strength is 4.0% ABV. This is one of seven cask beers regularly produced by the brewery. In addition to the regular brews there are over sixty special ales that are produced for different occasions. At the time of writing a special brew has been issued to celebrate the 75th anniversary of the Cave Rescue Organisation that is based in the Yorkshire Dales. A donation to the rescue team is given for every pint sold. What name have Dent Brewery given to this beer? "RescEWE". What else could they have called it?

Upon reaching Lea Yeat Bridge just before the village of Cowgill the path takes to the country again. I could continue to walk along the road all the way to Dent but decide to keep to my original plan in order to add some variety. My chosen route leads me through a network of narrow wooden footbridges that cross the numerous small tributary streams. The path threads its way through a succession of pastures with its route twisting so much that I begin to lose any sense of where I am relative to the river.

I mentioned earlier that I had not been conscious of any noticeable difference coming from Yorkshire into Cumbria. However, while striding through these riverside pastures it gradually dawns on me that there is a significant difference. The dry-stone walls have vanished. In their place the fields are now divided mostly by hedgerows. I later discovered that the reason for this difference is that Dentdale was one of the last areas in the country to be "enclosed", (the Act covering this area not being passed until 1859) and at that time hedges were more commonly used to form the divisions rather than walls.

My path eventually rejoins the bank of the River Dee and I walk alongside it as it as it sweeps me towards Church Bridge. On reaching the bridge it is time to take another short diversion and visit the charming village of Dent that lays only a short distance to my left.

Dent

Dent is the sort of place that attracts people in their droves to explore the narrow cobbled streets and take in the atmosphere. Unusually this is not the case today and I seem to have the delights of Dent all to myself. The public car park is usually overflowing with visitor's cars, but today I find that there is just a single solitary vehicle sitting among the myriad puddles. A blue Ford Escort where the lone occupant has been patiently waiting to see if this bedraggled walker is going to call it a day here and buy her a nice lunch, or continue walking for the afternoon (after buying her a nice lunch).

The small town is quite a little gem. Sheltered by the sides of the valley it is a close community of stone cottages and narrow cobbled streets. Apart from a few coats of paint and the coming of the electric light the streets are probably little different now than they were many years ago. The town is steeped in history and uncovering some of this is going to take me a lot longer than I had originally anticipated.

Dent has been a real hub of activity ever since Norman times. The church of St. Andrew dates from the 12th century although it has had at least four major renovations since then. Up until the 1930's Dent was a hive of different activities and local businesses, but now it is highly dependent upon tourism for its local income.

Early Dentdale was a key producer of wool. In the Middle Ages the owners of the land, the Cistercian Monks of Fountain Abbey, generated so much wealth from the production of wool that they reputedly became the richest monastery in England. Following the Dissolution of the Monasteries by Henry VIII in 1536 the production of wool became more localised so that the residents of Dent had easier access to the raw material. Dent became famous for its woollen garments and they were widely distributed. The industry peaked in the 18th and 19th centuries and then entered a steady decline as the 20th century progressed.

The Terrible Knitters of Dent

I expect most people would have some reservations about purchasing a woollen garment that they had been informed had been handmade by a terrible knitter. However you would be wrong, because these were not terrible knitters as in awful and incompetent, but "Terrible" as in "fast and furious". The "Terrible Knitters of Dent" was the term given to the local people who would spend every spare moment knitting quality garments to augment their income.

Almost everyone in Dent knitted in order to supplement their wages. Both women and men would knit every time they sat down to rest from their other labours. Many would also continue to knit as they walked to work. Their productivity was extraordinary and hand-knitted gloves, socks, scarves and pullovers were turned out at a phenomenal rate. Reports from those days claim that the terrible knitters could make their needles move at such a speed that they became a mere blur to the casual observer.

The "terrible knitters" were great practitioners of what we would now call multi-tasking. Some developed a unique skill so that they could keep knitting whilst going about their other jobs. A knitting needle would be fixed into a wooden holder that was carried on a belt around the waist, and the second needle would be worked furiously with the right hand. This technique meant that the left hand was free to carry out other tasks such as whilst working in the dairy or kitchen. I came across one tale of a herdsman who was reputed to be able to knit socks with one hand whilst milking a cow with the other!

Demand for Dent knitwear reached its peak during the Napoleonic Wars when the army and navy had an insatiable demand for warm clothing.

The last of the recognised "Terrible Knitters" was Elizabeth (Betty) Hartley who passed away in 2007 at the good age of 93 years. Betty had spent many of her later years displaying her traditional skills at schools and country fairs. With her passing an era of history for the people of Dent came to a close.

It was time for lunch in the Sun Inn. The Sun is a lovely old pub with its wooden-beamed ceilings and welcoming fire blazing in the hearth. The landlord serves an excellent lunch which I washed down with a couple of pints of Golden Fleece from the Dent Brewery. For the benefit of CAMRA purists this brew is a blonde beer rated at 3.7% ABV and possessing a light hoppy flavour.

I could not resist making the comment to my dearly beloved that she could have entered into the local spirit of the surroundings by knitting me a new pair of dry socks whilst eating her lunch. This jovial remark did not go down as well as it could have done.

Adam Sedgwick

There is a large pinkish-stone in the middle of the village that houses a drinking fountain. This impressive piece of granite is a memorial to Adam Sedgwick who is Dent's most distinguished son.

A stone is a very appropriate memorial because Adam Sedgwick's main claim to fame is that he is generally accepted as the founder of the science of geology.

Adam was the son of the local vicar and was born in Dent on 22nd March 1785. He spent his boyhood in the village and attended the local grammar school and later the nearby Sedberg School. His education was completed at Trinity College, Cambridge, where he was a distinguished and well respected student.

The academic world in those days was a very different place to the one we know today. Professorships were awarded to men of intelligence and academic standing, but they did not necessarily have to prove that standing in the specified subject. So it was that in 1818 Adam Sedgwick found himself elected to the Woodwardian Professorship of Geology at Cambridge University.

Geology was considered a new science and there was much for the enthusiastic new professor to discover. Sedgwick threw himself into his researches with great vigour. His early researches involved him taking many field trips and he was soon seen as being very much a leading light in this new science. Some of Sedgwick's greatest contributions to geological knowledge were made early in his career. These discoveries principally concerned the correct aging of rock formations, particularly for specimens from the Devonian era.

Sedgwick's researches were not without controversy. In 1827 he set off on an exploration trip to Western Scotland with fellow geologist Roderick Murchison. They worked together successfully on this project, but their joint interest in the aging of rocks was to later develop into one of the most spectacular fallouts in scientific history. During their different researches both men came up with the notion that some of the formations they were studying had been formed earlier than anyone had previously thought possible. Murchison named these rocks as Silurian after the Silurian Tribe that inhabited the Welsh Border area where he had first made his discovery. Sedgwick for his part claimed that he had found even older rocks from an even earlier era of up to 570 million years ago. These rocks he christened as Cambrian after the ancient Welsh tribe of Cambria. The two men argued publicly for years about who had discovered the oldest rocks. It was not simply the naming of the rocks that was important to each of the men; it was the recognition that it was him who had discovered the most ancient rock that drove them in their constant arguments with each other. Eventually it was Sedgwick who was recognized as the most prominent, and he went on to become a Fellow of the Royal Society and also President of the British Geological Society.

Sedgwick also found himself involved in another major controversy that also became very emotive. One of his earlier pupils was the young Charles Darwin who Sedgwick had taken on a field trip to Wales in 1831. The two men developed a close friendship that continued when Darwin set off on his famous Beagle Expedition. Darwin would send geological samples back to Sedgwick for him to examine in his Cambridge laboratory. This time it was nothing as trivial as the naming and aging of rocks that eventually split the two men apart. Theirs was not an argument about ego, but something altogether much, much deeper.

Sedgwick was a religious man who also had a strong belief in divine creation and catastrophism. To his mind the world had been shaped by sudden violent events through the ages, and not gradual changes. He also fervently believed that new species had been put on the world by divine order in a strict and meaningful sequence. You can therefore imagine what effect the publication of Darwin's "The Origin of the Species" had on their relationship. Sedgwick was vehemently opposed to any notion of the evolutionary process and remained firm in his conviction of divine creation for the rest of his life.

In other ways Sedgwick was way ahead of his time. As a lecturer at Cambridge he would welcome anyone into his sessions. He was one of the very first professors to encourage women to attend his lectures. In the early 19th century this was virtually unheard of. Sedgwick also later campaigned for Cambridge University to be opened up to non-Anglican students who had previously been excluded from studying there.

Adam Sedgwick died on January 27th 1873. Cambridge University named its geological museum in his honour and the

Sedgwick Museum is now incorporated into the Department of Earth Sciences. The Sedgwick Museum is open to the public.

Dent Village Heritage Centre

Before leaving Dent I really must visit the Dent Heritage Centre. The centre is an old petrol filling station has been converted into a village museum. It is packed to the rafters with artifacts from the olden days.

Visitors are taken back to times long ago, and the wealth of information available about the people who lived in this area is absolutely staggering. Many of the items on display are from the personal collection of Jim and Margaret Taylor who founded the centre. They have spent many years building up the collection and there are all sorts of bits and pieces on display.

The old forecourt contains old farm vehicles, and in the garage are old cars, fuel pumps and tools.

The inside is amazing. There are room displays laid out as the people would have lived in a bygone era. A kitchen, pantry and parlour are all filled with fascinating items. Information boards are everywhere with some most extraordinary facts about the daily habits and customs of those earlier inhabitants of Dentdale.

The kitchen was a place almost unrecognizable to our way of life and very unlike anything we have today. No fancy double-ovens and hobs in those days. The room was dominated by the fireplace which would have a water-boiler on one side and an oven on the other. Most of the cooking would have been carried out in a pot held above the flames by a hook. A wooden dolly-tub and washboard was the nearest thing that they had to a washing machine.

Another thing that was completely unknown to the people of that time was refrigerators and freezers. There was still a necessity to preserve food and this was carried out by bottling fruit and salting meat. One exhibit contains all the information you could ever require to preserve a pig in salt. Different amounts of salt were required to be rubbed into the parts of the meat depending on its type and the length of storage time. Different parts of the pig were then stored in different ways. It was a skilled job and there were specialist pig-killers and salters that would carry out the job. How did they learn all of that stuff in the first place? They couldn't simply "Google" pig preservation and print it out. Running a household was very demanding and the knowledge and skills were passed down from mother to daughter.

There was no HD flat-screen TV either. Evening entertainment was usually some form of handiwork, which for most of the workers of Dent meant just one thing; knitting.

In the cellar there is a reconstruction of part of the Settle-Carlisle railway around the Arten Gill viaduct. The model was constructed by model railway enthusiast Brian Irwin.

Throughout the museum there are numerous information sheets and time just flew by as I discovered many fascinating snippets about life in old Dentdale. There were so many interesting snippets that I nearly missed this next one. I am indebted to the curator of the museum who related this tale to me saying that it was just the sort of thing to include in my book because it was a unique story connecting Dent to Liverpool. It is the story of the "Cowmen of Dent" and here it is.

After the Napoleonic Wars had ended the demand for Dent knitwear noticeably declined and the townspeople urgently needed to find an extra source of income. Sometime around the year 1830 a group of the people of Dent decided that their future prosperity lay in the production of milk that they would sell to the city dwellers in order to boost their earnings.

Plans were made, investors sought and somehow the money was put together to buy a small dairy herd. Adventurously the group did not want to rely on local cows; they were going to invest in the finest dairy cows from Ireland. A party of the men folk duly set off to Liverpool where their intended mission was to purchase top quality dairy cows imported from Ireland and take them back to Dent to set up the new dairy farm. When they arrived in Liverpool everything initially proceeded according to plan and they successfully acquired the Irish dairy cows. At this point somebody had their "bright idea" and through some amazing "blue-skies" thought process came to the reasoning that now they owned the cows, why should they go to all of the bother of taking them all the way back to Dent only to send all of the milk back to Liverpool. Why not keep the cows in Liverpool?

Once their thought processes were on this tack there was just no stopping them. The minor matter that there were no fields for grazing the cows did not deter them one jot. They simply rented some empty houses and put the cows in them. The cattle-feed was shipped in to the city from Dent by cart and the cowmen simply sent the manure back out again on the same wagon. Everyone was a winner. The people of Liverpool were able to buy fresh milk, the people of Dent had their additional income and the cows were spared the long drove to Dent and were able to live in a comfortable shelter from the elements.

Apparently this enterprise ran for some time and the houses became known as "dairies" What a wonderful tale of ingenuity and opportunism. Goodness only knows what Liverpool Council said when they found out about it.

How much of this tale was 100% true and how much was a "wind-up" by the curator to add some fun to a quiet afternoon I will leave you to decide. All I will say is that the story was told well and I would not be surprised if there are not many more such tales that regularly bring a smile to visitors' faces.

I could have stayed chatting all day, but there are still a few more miles to cover today. It is time to say my goodbyes and promise to include the "Cowmen of Dent" in my book.

Dent to Millthrop

It is a very short distance from Dent village to Barth Bridge and I can continue my journey along the banks of the River Dee. The path continues to pull me through the lush meadows. Actually they could be mistaken for water meadows at the moment, because the rains are causing the ground to become waterlogged and there is a lot of surface water sloshing around.

Along this section I find one of those delightful little unexpected extras that add a bonus to life. The gateposts are sporting a small metal plaque about four inches square with raised relief images on them. I have found the "Network of Gates", an environmental art work compiled by Leeds-based artist Alan Pergusey. The route starts at Barth Bridge and follows the south bank up to Ellers Bridge, and then crosses the river to make the return journey. The work was commissioned by the Yorkshire Dales National Park Authority and the Yorkshire Dales Millennium Trust.

Passing through each gate I am enthralled by the succession of images. Flowers, fossils, tractors, and raindrops falling from the clouds are among the simple but enchanting relief works on display. There are 28 plates in all, and are scattered along this two-mile walk along the side of the River Dee.

Alan Pergusy specialises in art projects to enhance the environment and this little gem was his inspiration for celebrating the Millennium. The artist worked with the pupils, parents and staff at Dent Community Primary School to create the plaques. The images were compiled by the children which gives the designs an air of innocence and simplicity. Each design was carefully modeled with clay and then cast in gunmetal to give the final plaque.

It is a different experience threading my way through the "Network of Gates". I cannot help but wonder what little piece of delight is waiting for me at the next gateway and I find myself scurrying along from plaque to plaque until I come to the end of this particular trail.

Below Ellers Bridge the path continues along the flat valley floor. I eventually reach a footbridge to cross the river at Brackensgill. A prayer of gratitude needs to be offered at this point because until 1999 the crossing would have been by means of a ford across the river. This would not have been a bundle of laughs today with the water-levels high and still rising with the rainfall.

It is time to leave the River Dent behind and contour around to Millthrop where I will pick up the River Rawthey. That is not the only geographical feature that I will be leaving behind. The familiar light-coloured limestone has also disappeared to be replaced by dour grey slate. This sharp transformation is the result of the "Dent Fault" where the fault-line cuts off the limestone beds and exposes the slate beds of lower Dentdale. So in a short distance the landscape is transformed from the Dales to be more like that of the Lake District. It is not only the landscape that changes, but the appearances of the buildings as well. Nearly all of the buildings were originally constructed from locally available materials with a result that the honey-toned limestone cottages of the Dales take on the more harsh dark grey of austere granite.

I take a last long and lingering look back at Dentdale and then turn towards the outline of the Howgills in the distance. Next stop Sedbergh.

Sedbergh School

Sedbergh is not an exact destination on the Dales Way. Instead of passing through the town the trail makes its journey down the River Rawthey and then along the bank of the River Lune. This takes the walker on a curved route around Sedbergh that would make a 5 o'clock to 10 o'clock sweep if it was viewed on a map.

The circular route provides some excellent walking through pastures dotted with sycamore, hawthorn and ash trees. The first few minutes from Millthrop are spent wandering beneath a broad-leaved canopy providing some welcome shelter from the elements.

Back into the open again, and the path cuts over the edges of the playing fields of Sedbergh School. These playing fields have been trodden by far more celebrated feet than my own size nines. No less than three England rugby union captains first learned their skills on these fields. They are Wavell Wakefied, John Spencer and Will Carling. Needless to say the school puts a great value on sport and has an impressive list of former pupils who have excelled at the highest level.

Sedbergh School was founded in 1525 by Roger Lupton who was the Provost of Eton College. Lupton was born in nearby Cautley in 1456 and established the school to benefit his home area. It was originally established as a Chantry School and the foundation deed attaches Sedbergh to St. John's College, Cambridge. The school was re-established as a grammar school in 1551.

The fortunes of the school rose and fell until the early 19th century when it went through something of a slump, with only eight boys on the roll at one time. All this changed with the appointment of John Harrison Evans as headmaster in 1838. Evans drove the school forward with his enthusiasm and its reputation quickly spread. Successive headmasters continued the expansion by adding more buildings to further develop the facilities.

The school motto is *"Dura Virum Nutrix"* which translates as "A Stern Nurse of Men". A fitting motto, for the school had a reputation for the "early morning run and cold showers" style of regime which was still in existence until the late 1960's.

It would be remiss not to make a mention of the school's memorial cloisters. The cloisters were dedicated in 1924 to the memory of all of the Old Sedberghians who gave their lives in the Great War. After the Second World War the cloisters were rededicated to include those who had fallen during that conflict as well. The cloisters display the names of all of the men who perished during those hostilities.

There is also a separate special memorial to the Old Sedberghians who were awarded the highest medal for gallantry, the

Victoria Cross. The four distinguished gentlemen are; Robert James Thomas Digby-Jones, Royal Engineers (Wagon Hill 1900), George Ward Gunn, Royal Horse Artillery (Sidi Razegh 1941), John Charles Campbell, 7th Armoured Division (Sidi Razegh 1941), Kenneth Campbell, Royal Air Force, (Brest Harbour 1941)

The school is open to both girls and boys and would appear to offer a fine foundation for young people.

Sedbergh

Although Sedbergh is not officially on the Dales Way it provides an excellent place for a visit, so I will take a look at the history of the town before resuming my planned route.

Sedbergh derives its name from the Norse language where it was called Set Burgh, which translates as a flat-topped hill. The town is old and is situated in one of those geographical locations where a town simply has to become established. Everything about the lay of the land screams out for a settlement. It sits at the confluence of four river valleys and is sheltered by the Howgills to the north, Firbank Fell to the west and Holme Fells and Frostrow Fells to the south. Ancient track routes tended to follow the valleys and so consequently settlements would develop where these routes crossed. Such locations were ideal for markets and this is where Sedberg started to come to prominence.

In early days there was no such thing as an open market for exchange of goods. All markets had to be approved by a charter authorized by the King himself. In the same way that Tesco cannot just open a new supermarket wherever they want to today, so merchants in those long-gone days could not simply set their stalls up wherever they fancied either. Somebody had to apply to the King to be able to set up a lawful market.

Henry III granted Sedbergh a market charter in 1251. Unfortunately some poor civil servant at one point let it lapse and a second charter was approved by Henry VIII in 1538. The market is still held today and there is a plaque on the library wall commemorating the original charter.

Sedbergh celebrates its market rather more than happens in some other towns. In August the town holds its annual market to commemorate the original charter. On this day the streets are full of stalls and street entertainers are seen performing for the crowds. To keep in the spirit of the occasion everyone is encouraged to wear old English costumes which add some extra colour to the occasion.

In its early days the town of Sedbergh was overshadowed by its near neighbour Dent. The knitting industry was more firmly established in Dent and therefore the economy was more advanced than in Sedbergh. This was all to change with the passing of the Turnpike Acts of 1761. The implementation of the Acts stimulated tremendous improvements to be made to the roads linking Askrigg to Kendal and Lancaster to Kirkby-Stephen. Both of these new turnpikes crossed at Sedbergh and the town started to grow as a result of the increased traffic. The introduction of cotton mills at Howgill and Millthrop further increased the level of trade in the town and Sedbergh started to steadily outstrip Dent until it become the dominant town of the area.

Sedbergh is the largest town within the Yorkshire Dales National Park having a population of just under 4,000 people. Not so long ago Sedbergh was part of the West Riding of Yorkshire but the boundary changes of 1974 placed the town in the new county of Cumbria where it has remained ever since.

Sedbergh Book Town

It is a more recent change that has elevated the status of Sedbergh and placed it firmly on the map. A very simple idea has transformed the local economy and is a shining example of what can be achieved with a combination of some inspired thinking and community spirit.

For many years Sedbergh School was the major source of employment and the only other major contributor to the local economy in the late 20th century was tourism. This depended almost entirely on people coming to walk in the Howgills or the Dales.

All this came to a sudden dramatic stop with the outbreak of foot-and-mouth disease in 2001. The farmers quite understandably closed off all of the footpaths with the walkers equally understandably cancelling their bookings. The town was thrown into a state of despair. It is in such times of adversity that strength of character comes to the fore and instead of sitting around bemoaning their lot the good people of Sedbergh decided that they needed to do something about it.

I don't know exactly how anyone's brain leaps from closed footpaths to shops full of second-hand books but somebody's brain did just that. Sedbegh developed itself into a "book town", one of only three in the UK. The original concept was the brainchild of book-dealer Richard Booth who established Hay-on-Wye as the very first book-town in 1961. There are now three such towns in the Uk, and a total of thirteen around the world. The three in Britain are Hay-on-Wye, Sedbergh and Wigtown which is in South-west Scotland.

There are bookshops everywhere, and in addition to those there are various publishing, binding and restoring workshops to service and support their requirements. The industry boomed and became established so quickly that in the short space of time since the disastrous foot-and-mouth outbreak the book business has overtaken the school as the largest source of employment in the area.

A company was founded in 2003 to develop the theme and given the name of "Sedbergh Book Town". The effect was spectacular and the town of Sedbergh has not turned back any pages since. Books are readily available covering every conceivable subject and specialist outlets abound. For anyone who loves books Sedbergh is a paradise and browsers can be found in every outlet searching for that much-desired volume that has been missing from their lives for so long. This has been something of a revolution for the town and books have become a great success story for the people of Sedbergh. Hats off to them.

The Search For A Twin

Following the great success of the venture into the book business the townspeople of Sedbergh decided to embark on a further adventure. They came to the conclusion that what Sedbergh really needed to do next was to find itself a "twin".

Deciding that you want to find a twin and actually finding a suitable candidate are two entirely different propositions. It is rather similar to the personal dating scene where you have to kiss a lot of frogs before one eventually turns into a handsome prince, and then only if you are very lucky. Sedbergh decided that it could do without all of this hassle and opted for its own version of "speed dating".

The town volunteered to take part in a BBC2 "real life" documentary entitled "The Town That Wants a Twin" that was broadcast in January 2005. During September and October 2004 the people of Sedbergh were exposed to the various merits of four continental towns, Eymet (France), Athienov (Cyprus), Zrece (Slovenia) and Seefeld (Austria) in full view of the cameras.

After all of the various exploratory visits had been completed the town held an election to decide which of the contenders they wished to have as their new twin. People enthusiastically campaigned for their favourites with speeches, rallies and posters. So popular was the competition that the turn-out for the poll was greater than the typical response for general or council elections.

The clear winner of the "twin referendum" was the Slovenian town of Zrece. It was an overwhelming decision with more votes being cast for Zrece than the other three candidates combined.

The people of Sedbergh had found their twin.

Brigflatts and George Fox

Many years ago in the mid 17th century there was a quiet revolution in the Yorkshire Dales. This was a different type of change to the various industrial developments that we have previously taken a look at during this journey. These were social changes and were the source of much antagonism with the Church authorities. The catalyst for these changes was a gentleman by the name of George Fox.

I must admit that I had not previously heard of Fox until I commenced this walk, but along the way I have already passed several buildings that would not be standing if it were not for his teachings. George Fox was one of the major founders of the Society of Friends, more commonly referred to as the Quakers.

George Fox was the eldest child of a weaver and was born in July 1624 in the village of Drayton-le-Clay, Leicestershire. (The village is presently known by the name of Fenny Drayton). The village had a strong puritan nature and his father, Christopher Fox, was known as "Righteous Christer" by his neighbours.

From an early age young George developed a serious and contemplative disposition, and it was thought that he would eventually turn to the priesthood. However, George began his early adulthood as an apprentice to a local shoemaker and grazier. He became increasingly contemplative and obsessed with the simplicity of life, dismissing the values of wealth and ownership. This caused him some considerable turmoil in his thoughts, and at the age of nineteen he set off to travel in an attempt, as we would say today, to "find himself".

On his travels Fox sought out clergymen with whom he would discuss religious topics. He also made a number of contacts with groups of "English Dissenters" who had broken away from the teachings of the mainstream Church of England. The cumulative effects from these various contacts and discussions began to form into his own set of beliefs, which slowly became the foundations for his own preaching. The basis of Fox's teachings was that every person has an equal value, that everyone has something of God in them and that people should act with a sense of responsibility for the greater good. He strongly believed that pacifism and harmonious living was the right way forward for the development of the human race and that people should always act in the way that best achieves the "common good". More controversially Fox spread the message that there was no after-life redemption as promised by traditional Christian teachings, and life had to be lived in the present. This was more than enough to upset the Church authorities, but the part of George Fox's teachings that really enraged some quarters was his conviction that priests and religious rituals formed an obstruction between man and God and that they were totally unnecessary.

As you can imagine Fox's teachings did not go down well with the Establishment of the day. If you also add in that he also taught that men and women were equal before God (remember this was 350 years before Mrs. Pankhurst and the Suffragettes) and did not recognize the authority of appointed magistrates then you can easily see how Fox rapidly became a thorn in the side of the "Powers-that-be". Inevitably this led to Fox being arrested and imprisoned on a regular basis. On one such occasion Fox famously told a magistrate that he did not recognize the court's authority and would only "Quake with fear before God". This is believed to be the origins of how the name "Quakers" was derived to describe the movement.

The years that George Fox spent travelling and preaching gradually produced a band of followers. The folk of the Yorkshire Dales were generally a quiet, introspective and contemplative breed of people and found that Fox's teachings were in harmony with their own thoughts. Over a thousand people were in attendance when Fox gave an oration on nearby Firbank Fell. The part of the fell where this occurred is still known as "Fox's Pulpit".

Fox meanwhile spent several more terms in prison for his beliefs. In 1671 he travelled to America and spent two years there spreading his message and taking a great interest in the development of the State of Pennsylvania. The State was being founded and established using Quaker principles by his friend William Penn. Fox considered his work across the Atlantic completed and returned to England satisfied that his message was being accepted in the new colonies. He then turned his attentions to the people of mainland Europe, particularly those in the Netherlands.

Back in England the non-conformist followers were still being constantly persecuted by the authorities. Their meetings were banned and thousands of Quakers were arrested and imprisoned. This persecution was to continue until King James II finally agreed to pardon the dissenters. However, it was not until after the Glorious Revolution of 1688 and the passing of the Act of Toleration in 1689 that the Quaker movement was permitted to progress unhindered.

George Fox continued to promote his teachings until the end of his life. He died on 13th January 1691, having lived long enough to see the Society that he had worked so hard to found finally released from its persecution. Fox is buried in the Non-Conformists Burial Ground in Burnhill Fields, London. There is a memorial to him that can be found at his birthplace in Fenny Drayton, Leicestershire. The largest memorial to his name is the George Fox University in Newberg, Oregon, USA.

So that is the story of George Fox but what has it to do with the small cluster of buildings that I am now approaching at

Brigflatts? Well, it was here that George Fox came in June 1652 looking to make contact with a group known as the "Westmorland Seekers". Specifically he was looking to find a gentleman by the name of Richard Robinson who was considered to be the leader of the group and who lived nearby. After his meeting with Robinson Fox set off to give his famous oration on Firbank Fell.

Fox had some while earlier claimed to have received a vision that revealed to him a Meeting House standing by the side of a river, and when he first set eyes on Brigflatts he knew that this was the right place. Meetings have been regularly held at Brigflatts ever since.

Quakerism swept through the area and many meeting houses were constructed. There are several along the Dales Way including the one at Brigflatts where I am passing through now. Brigflatts itself is a small collection of less than a dozen buildings, but one white lime-washed cottage particularly stands out. This is the Meeting House and was constructed in 1675. In those days it was illegal to attend non-conformist meetings so feelings must have been very strong for the locals to declare their affinity in such a bold manner.

The Brigflatts Meeting House is considered to be one of the most important Quaker buildings in England. It receives more than 2,000 visitors every year. The initial construction was built by the local people and it has undergone several renovations since it was first established. It is now a Grade I listed building. Visitors are always welcome, and weekly meetings are held every Sunday.

Shortly after Brigflatts the way leads across the pastureland and contours around the hill before dropping down to the Rive Lune at Lincolns Inn Bridge. The bridge itself is a lovely double-arched stone construction and straddles the river forming an excellent picture with the waters flowing briskly below. I did wonder if there was any connection to Lincolns Inn in London, but apparently not. The name originated from a local inn that has since been converted to a farmhouse. The owner of the inn at one time was known as Lincoln. Such was his popularity of the hostelry that it became known simply as "Lincoln's Inn" and the name has stuck ever since.

Lincoln's Inn Bridge is the end of my travels for today. The weather has brightened up and I am able to sit comfortably on the bank contemplating the waters and all of the things I have learned during the previous few hours as I wait for my transport back to the B&B.

DAY FIVE

LINCOLNS INN BRIDGE TO BURNESIDE

13.3 MILES

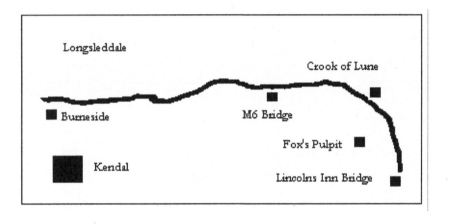

Lincolns Inn Bridge to Crook of Lune

Yippeee!

The rain has stopped and the sun is shining.

Everywhere is wet and soggy which will mean that there will

be a lot of squelching, slipping and sliding as I move along the path today, but at least I will be able to tuck the hood away and enjoy an unrestricted view of the surroundings.

Today will also be different in that the walk does not pass any settlements of any size, the closest that I am going to get will be the odd farmhouse dotted along my route. In a way it will be the most isolated section of the walk. Coming "over the top" at Cam House was only a relatively short distance before reaching Dent, but today will be more than twice that distance before I eventually reach the village of Burneside.

It is with a cheery smile that I set off from Lincolns Inn Bridge to enjoy the delights of the Lune Valley. The river is carrying a good head of water following the downpours and is surging down its course and creating its own soundtrack to the view unfolding before me.

Crosdale Beck is my first challenge of the day. This feeder stream cuts across my path before joining the main waterway. The stream is running much higher than normal and I can only just make out the stepping stones that are submerged two or three inches below the surface. On either side of the stones it is evident that the water was considerably deeper and the odds looked to favour a boot-full of water at the very least. At this point I could choose to "wimp-out" and follow the alternative path that crosses the stream a lot higher up the hillside. Indeed to the sensible walker with a full day ahead it would be the obvious selection. However, my courage is fortified with the knowledge that I had a dry pair of socks in the rucksack if the worst came to the worst. I stepped boldly on to the slippery crossing. Steady........a slight wobble.........and..........over! Safe and I still have dry feet. Murphy's Law would have inevitably ensured that without the spare socks I would have plunged my foot right into the hole, but with the knowledge that the insurance was literally in the bag I was able to complete the operation without mishap.

The route then passes below a tall viaduct that once carried the railway. It is another beautiful example of Victorian engineering and a great pity that it is no longer in use. After passing underneath the viaduct the footpath turns uphill to take a higher route enabling me to look down at the river below. I can also see across the valley to Fox's Pulpit and Firbank Fell. I enjoy twenty minutes or so sauntering along this upper trail before descending again to the River Lune.

I am at the Westward end of the Howghills with the main tops rising to my right and the summit of Winder straight ahead. The Howgills are not a very well-known range of hills, but offer some very attractive walks. Only the southern parts of the range are within the boundaries of the Dales National Park. The hills generally have a "humpy" appearance rather than the sharper peaks of most of the Pennines which prompted the famous walker and writer Alfred Wainwright to once describe them as being like "A herd of sleeping elephants". They are made up of Ordovician and Silurian rocks rather than the carboniferous limestone of the Yorkshire Dales. The Howgills are not very high, with the highest summit of the range being "The Calf" at 676m closely followed by "Calders" at 674m.

Many people may be acquainted with the term "Munro" when applied to classifying the mountains of Scotland. The title is awarded to a Scottish mountain over 3000ft (914m) in height that is not considered to be part of another mountain. The name is given in tribute Sir Hugh Munro (1856 to 1919) who first published the complete list of 283 summits in 1891. Many walkers compete in "Munro Bagging" to climb as many as possible during their lifetime and over 4,000 people have claimed them all, including Stephen Pyke who climbed them all in a period of just 40 days.

All very well you say, but what does all that have to do with the Howgills? As I have already mentioned the peaks are not high enough to be classified in such grand terms as Munros, so the English had to think of a way of classifying our own hilltops. In true style of the ever-ironic and mickey-taking English sense of humour we came up with the "Marilyn". Think about it for a moment – peaks, mountains, Munro, Marilyn. Yes; you have made the connection.

The "Marilyn" is defined as any hill with a relative height to its surroundings of 150m (492 ft), regardless of its actual height. This gives us 2010 "Marilyns" in the British Isles,

Scotland	1216
Ireland	515
England	177

Using this means of classification the Howgills can claim to have two "Marilyns", "The Calf" and "Yarlside".

There is a further "claim to fame" to be found in these hills, and one that could come in handy some day at the local pub quiz. The Howgills are the proud owners of England's highest water fall. Cautley Spout has a drop of 178m which, although it is a long way short of the 979m height of the Angel Falls in Venezuela, is the best that our small island can do. The falls are on "The Calf" where the River Rawthey cascades over a cliff towards the head of a bleak valley. There are some who argue that England's highest waterfall is "Gaping Gill" on Ingleborough, where the fall drops into a pothole. However as most of the "Gaping Gill" waterfall is underground and Cautley Spout is all above ground, I will go along with Cautley as being the highest that we have.

The Howgills provide a fine skyline for this section of the walk, with their undulating humps continually attracting my eyes.

The Dales Way keeps tight to the river for the next mile, with an accompaniment of light woodlands. The path is very muddy and some careful navigation around some of the more boggy parts is required, particularly on the more steeply inclined banks. The trees and river combine to provide a very attractive part of the walk and it seems that all too quickly I arrive at the Crook of

Lune where my onward journey will take me back to open fields once more.

The bridge at Crook of Lune is a very attractive old double-arched packhorse bridge that is only just wide enough for a car to travel across it. In common with most bridges along the Dales Way it provides an excellent photograph and I duly honour it by taking a few snaps for my collection. It has been a marvelous start to the morning and it is now time to leave the riverside and strike out across open country again.

Shortly after the Crook of Lune there is another wonderful example of Victorian railway engineering. The Lowgill Viaduct spans the valley carrying the Tebay to Ingleton railway line high above the surrounding slopes.

Striding out over the open fields there is a solitude and peace that makes me feel as one with the world. After enjoying a very pleasant half-hour crossing the quiet pastures the peace and tranquility is rudely shattered by the unmistakable roar of the internal combustion engine and the dull monotonic rumble of heavy traffic. The soothing track of the Dales Way has brought me to the noise and diesel fumes of one of Britain's busiest motorways, the M6. A concrete footbridge takes me over this man-made scar on the landscape and I am able to look down at the constant streams of vehicles pouring their way north and south on its tarmac surface.

The M6 Motorway

Let us take a short time to consider the M6 Motorway. It is very easy to forget that this motorway was not exactly planned to be the great north-south link that it has become today. Rather it started its life as a series of short by-passes that gradually became joined up over half a century.

The first stage was the Preston Bypass, opened on 5th December 1958 by the Prime Minister, Harold MacMillan. It was the first stretch of motorway to be opened in Great Britain. So for your starter for ten, if the first motorway was opened in December 1958 then when was a section of that motorway first shut off for road works? Absolutely correct; January 1959. It only took a month for approximately 90m of road surface to become damaged and in urgent need of repair. In a manner somewhat similar to that which would later be used by Network Rail claiming "leaves on the line" or "wrong kind of snow" the bright managers at the Ministry of Transport blamed this one on the theory that the surface had been damaged by the unexpected effects of water falling on the road and then freezing and thawing. Rain and ice in the Lancashire hills in December – who would have thought it!

Many people today look at the M6 on a map and come to the quite logical conclusion that the road was built to offer a fast artery up the west side of the country while the M1 provided a similar route up the east side. That may have been the final result, but it was definitely not built that way. The motorway was constructed in little bits and then eventually linked up. This process took fifty years to complete. Anyone starting work in the Ministry of Transport planning office straight from school when the road was first on the drawing board would have retired before they could see the fruits of their labour.

The second stage of the M6 development was to extend the motorway in 1960 to include the Lancaster By-pass. Then in 1962, over 100 miles away to the south, the Stafford By-pass became the third part of the "join the dots" system to be completed. Various other stages were added over the years, but it was not until 1971 that the M6 became linked to the M1 by completing the section between Rugby and Castle Bromwich. It was still not complete then, because the northern end of the motorway was waving around unlinked at Carlisle, discharging its heavy flows on to the standard road system causing congestion. At the same time the A74(M) from Glasgow stopped a tantalizingly close 6 miles away at Gretna also causing traffic bottlenecks. Eventually common sense prevailed and on 5th December 2008, exactly 50 years after the first stretch at Preston was opened the motorway could finally be considered complete. The complete road covers 227 miles between Junction 19 of the M1 (now better known to listeners radio traffic reports as the Catthorpe Interchange), to the junction with the A74(M) at Gretna just north of the border with Scotland.

The M6 is almost always mentioned on radio traffic reports and has famous bottlenecks which will be familiar to all; Catthorpe Interchange, Spaghetti Junction, Walsall, Wolverhampton, Thelwall Viaduct and the M62 Junctions, all of which have regular traffic jams. None of this is very surprising when you consider that the original plans were for the motorway to cope with 72,000 vehicles per day, whereas today the volume of traffic is two and a half times that at 180,000 vehicles.

The traffic is flowing smoothly below me today so there is not quite that number of vehicles, but there are still an awful lot of them down there.

Onwards to Burneside

The next few miles consist of a steady stroll across the fields, dodging around coppices and fencing, and on and off various tracks and paths. The fields are a lot more open along this section and they are mostly divided by wire fences that produce very different scenery to the walls and hedgerows that decorated the countryside during the previous days.

It is a great change to be walking through such open fields after following up and down so many valleys over the previous days. The countryside is so very different now, gentle undulations replacing the more dramatic slopes of the Yorkshire Dales.

The path looks simple and straightforward on the map but on the ground it is very different in places. I find myself standing in a farmyard unsuccessfully looking this way and that for the way-marker. It is nowhere to be seen. I know where I want to go, but there is a gate across the track bearing a newly-painted sign announcing the ominous word "Private" in big letters. After a few minutes of looking at the map and pointing my compass at various distant landmarks in an attempt to verify that I was where I thought I was, a lady appears at the farmhouse door and asks if I am OK. After explaining my predicament the nice lady informs me that she often has to assist people looking for the footpath. She explained that I needed to go back a couple of fields and turn alongside a hedge, adding helpfully that there used to be a big sign at that turning point but "they" (whoever "they" are) had recently taken it away. Anyhow, the nice lady revealed that it would all be sorted out soon because "they" were going to erect some new signs over the next couple of weeks so that walkers would find their way better and not keep ending up in her farmyard. Trust me to choose this limbo period for my expedition.

The Dales Way continues through more and more open fields, twisting around hillocks and taking me on several occasions through some very muddy areas, particularly around Black Moss Tarn. There are plenty of sheep, and their bleating is often the only sound that can be heard as I steadily progress towards the end of my penultimate day.

So it was a fairly uneventful last stage to Burneside where I met up with "Dearly Beloved" for the drive to the B&B. It was only then that I realised how close this pleasant day had come to being a disaster.

"Just as well it didn't rain" she greeted me "You left your spare socks in the car".

A BREAK IN KENDAL

Kendal

Kendal is similar to Sedbergh in that it is not actually on the Dales Way, but sits adjacent to it. There are so many interesting things to see in Kendal that it is well worth taking the diversion to sample its delights.

The visitor can easily spend many hours simply wandering around and exploring the streets. The river provides a central corridor through the town and a pleasant walk up one bank and down the other between the main bridges. If all that is not enough then an invigorating walk up to the ruined castle reveals a panoramic view across Westmorland from the Dales to the more austere peaks of the Lake District.

The town of Kendal sits in the Kent valley, and the name is simply a corruption of Kent and Dale. The original settlers here were the Brigantes, and then the Romans settled here in the first century and built a fort at nearby Watercrook. When the Romans left Britain towards the end of the 4th century the area was left to its own devices until the Normans came and imposed the feudal system on the locality.

Kendal really started to develop as a trading post in 1189 when Richard I granted a market charter. King Richard was desperate to finance his crusades and granting charters and collecting the payments for them was one of his ways of raising much-needed funds.

The location of Kendal is such that it is quite close to Scotland, which has meant that the town has been subjected to many raids from marauding Scots over the ages. The worst instance occurred in 1210 when a band of looters led by the Earl of Fife descended upon Kendal killing many men, women and children in the process.

The wool industry prospered in Westmorland during the middle ages and Kendal became a key centre. It was particularly celebrated for the manufacture of "Kendal Green", a woollen cloth dyed in a particular shade of green that was in particular demand for clothing and blankets.

Kendal Green was the chosen uniform of the Kendal Bowmen, feared exponents of the English longbow who played a decisive role in the Battle of Flodden Field, the last battle on English soil where the use of the longbow played such a key part. The battle was fought on Flodden Field near to the Northumberland village of Branxton on September 9th 1513 between the Scottish forces of King James IV and the English led by Thomas Howard, Duke of Sussex. According to some sources this battle was the largest in terms of numbers fought between England and Scotland, with 24,000 English lined up against 34,000

Scots. The result was a resounding victory for the English, and the Scottish King was killed during the battle.

The layout of the town is somewhat unique. There is a main central road, Highgate, with narrow yards and lanes leading from it. Most of the buildings were built using the local grey limestone which adds a moody atmosphere. This feature has given Kendal the epithet of the "Auld Grey Town".

It is great fun to just wander around the centre of Kendal exploring all of the many yards. In Kendal a yard is a narrow lane or alley leading off the main street. Once these contained the various workshops with living space above, but have now been mostly renovated and "gentrified" into boutiques, shops and cottages. The yards are all numbered and named, the name usually relating to the owner of the building at the top of the yard. (E.g. Yard No 83 is known as Dr.Mannings Yard).

Wool was responsible for the major part of the wealth of Kendal for many years. New industries did spring up to replace the traditional ones, most notably for shoes and snuff.

Snuff

It is quite some time since I was last passed a snuff-box after a dinner. At one time it would have been a highly fashionable thing to have done, and marked a person as belonging to the "elite" who chose to take their tobacco fix in this manner rather than puff away on a ciggy. On thinking about it, it is somewhat surprising that snuff has not made a comeback as it would allow tobacco to be consumed at the table rather than having to vacate ones seat to take a quick drag out on the street.

Snuff taking has been known in Europe since the fifteenth century when it was discovered being used on Haiti during one of Christopher Columbus's voyages of discovery. It became very popular among the upper echelons of European society after Catherine de Medici claimed that it had medicinal properties. The taking of snuff was seen by many as a behaviour of the "elite" and Louis XIII, Queen Charlotte and even Pope Benedict XIII were among the "great and the good" who were users of snuff and helped to promote its use among their contemporaries.

Snuff is altogether a much more complex product than it would first appear. Initially I thought that snuff was simply snuff, a finely powdered tobacco. No, no, no, far from it. Snuff comes in a whole variety of textures and flavourings. Size varies from fine to coarse, which is relatively straightforward, but then it gets a lot more complicated. The dryness comes into consideration from the driest (which I am told is called "toast") to a moist product that is more usually applied to the gums rather than inhaled through the nose.

When it comes to flavours the subject becomes very complex. Traditional flavours were menthol, peppermint and spice, but the huge range of flavours available today covers every conceivable palette. Snuff is available in such flavours as aniseed, apple, apricot, lavender and I even found one described as wallflower!

What has all is got to do with Kendal? Well, as unlikely as it may seem the town is the home to one of the oldest companies in Britain, Samuel Gawith and Company, and it's flagship product is snuff.

It all came about in 1792 when an enterprising young man named Thomas Harrison left his native Kendal to learn all about the process for manufacturing snuff. He had identified snuff as the product of the future and intended to make his fortune from it. Harrison went to Glasgow and learned everything he could from the manufacturers in that city. Not only did he learn what to do, but he also acquired several cartloads of second-hand manufacturing equipment that have more than paid for themselves ever since. So good was this machinery that some of it is still working today! Yes; one of the original machines is still producing snuff at the factory today. The magazine "Design and Components in Industry" claimed that it was the oldest machinery still in use, and that was back in 1965. Some Scotsman is probably still looking down from above wishing that he had been aware of how long a life the old equipment he was selling on to the Englishman was going to enjoy. He would no doubt have charged Thomas Harrison a "wee bit more" for it.

Harrison soon had the manufacturing processes working effectively and producing quality snuff. He entered into a partnership with a local chemist, Thomas Brocklebank, who sold the finished products in his pharmacy.

On his passing Thomas Harrison left the business to his son, who was also named Thomas. The business continued to prosper and it is when we come to January 1838 that things started to get a little more interesting. Thomas had a daughter, Jane, who had fallen madly in love with a local plumber, one Samuel Gawith. Harrison did not approve of this liaison, and so in true romantic fashion Samuel and Jane ran off to Gretna Green and married against her father's wishes. There must have been some reconciliation because when Thomas Harrison passed away in 1841 the business was left between Jane, her elder sister Ann and Thomas Brocklebank.

Samuel Gawith left his own trade and joined in at the snuff factory, learning all about the workings of the snuff trade. With the passing of the aging Brocklebank and the early death of Ann, the factory passed into the hands of Samuel Gawith in 1852. The company continued to prosper under Samuels's leadership and was becoming a leading employer in Kendal. Gawith was elected Mayor of Kendal in 1864 and unfortunately this was to be his last happy achievement. His beloved wife Jane died later that same year, and Gawith himself followed only a short time afterwards.

The snuff business was left in the hands of three trustees; Samuels own son, Samuel the Second, Henry Hogarth a surveyor and friend of Samuel the First, and John Illingworth, who had spent ten years at the company and was the main commercial traveler.

Illingworth later set up his own snuff and tobacco company that was to survive in Kendal for more than a century until it was taken over by Joseph Wilsons in the late 1980's.

Many family concerns have their problems when some of the relatives believe that they could do better, and the Gawith dynasty were no exception. John Gawith who had been helping his elder brother Samuel the Second to build the business had a series of disagreements with his sibling and the two men decided that things would be better if they divided the business and went their separate ways. This they did, but John was not as skilled in the ways of business as Samuel and he became over-stretched and finally became insolvent. Samuel re-acquired the trademarks of his brother's business and absorbed them back into his own.

At the same time as John Gawith's breakaway concern was coming to an end, their youngest brother William also decided to make a break from the family business. William had married the sister of Henry Hogarth and set up in partnership with him. This venture was rather more successful than that of his brother John, and the firm is still successfully trading today as "Gawith Hoggarth TT".

So that is how Kendal became known for it's snuff and I am reliably informed that "Kendal Brown" is a much sought after product among the aficionados of snuff taking. Thomas Harrison's legacy lives on, which unlike his product is not something to be sniffed at.

The Quaker Tapestry

During the seventeenth and eighteenth centuries several Quaker and Methodist families became prominent in the local community. I have previously mentioned George Fox and the way that the people of the Dales found sympathy with his preaching. This was also notable in Kendal and the first Friends meeting House was erected in 1688. The current meeting house stands on the same site and was built in 1816. It is an elegant Georgian building and houses a unique set of tapestries known as the Quaker Tapestry.

The tapestries are a collection of 77 narrative panels each 21 inches high and 25 inches wide, depicting the story of Quakerism over its 350 year history. Although known as a tapestry, the craftwork should be more accurately referred to as embroidery. The panels are constructed with a technique known as "crewel embroidery" which uses wool stitched into a canvas using a design pre-drawn on the material surface. This is a similar method to that used in the construction of the Bayeaux Tapestry several hundred years previously.

The inspiration for the embroidery came from school teacher Anne Wynne-Wilson (1926 – 1998). One day during one of her lessons a young boy made a casual comment that a lot of things were made clearer to him by looking at pictures. This struck a chord with Anne, and she set about thinking about how her Quaker beliefs could be represented in illustrative form. Anne was also an enthusiastic and accomplished embroiderer and set about representing some of the Quaker history and beliefs in her embroidery. At a Friends meeting in 1982 Anne presented an exhibition of her "work in progress". Everyone present was impressed both by the work itself and the sentiments behind it, but also the sheer enthusiasm portrayed by Anne Wynne-Wilson to develop her vision.

Before very long the project was fully under way. Design teams were set up and groups of Friends from around the world put their names forward to craft the different panels. Many of the willing volunteers had no previous experience of embroidery, so workshops had to be organised to train these new enthusiasts. In all over 4000 people in 15 different countries made a contribution to the project. The Tapestries were finally completed in 1996.

The finished work is not simply a narrative of the history and beliefs of the movement, but also a celebration of the great achievements of some of its members. For example I was not previously aware that John Dalton whose genius gave us modern atomic theory was of Quaker beliefs.

The exhibition of the tapestries are open to the public Mondays to Fridays, with occasional Saturdays and Bank Holiday openings.

Kendal Mint Cake

Most people have heard of Kendal Mint Cake even if they have never actually tasted it. This confection is the original high-energy food. Forget the others, this is true calorific dynamite and always features prominently on any list of "emergency rations" for those venturing out into the great outdoors.

There are various claims for the invention, but the one generally agreed to be correct is that Kendal Mint Cake was first produced in 1869 by Joseph Wiper while he was conducting some experiments in his sweet workshop. Wiper was attempting to perfect the manufacture of clear glacier mints. What he ended up with on this particular occasion was a hard opaque substance with an extremely sweet taste. Wipers christened it "Kendal Mint Cake" and a new industry was born.

From its early days Kendal Mint Cake was recognised as a source of energy. Ernest Shackleton took supplies of Kendal Mint Cake with him on his great Transarctic Expedition of 1914 to 1917. The bars became a regular feature on many expeditions, but the sales really went into overdrive following the first ascent of Mount Everest in 1953. Sir Edmund Hilary vividly described the sensations he felt with Tensing Norgay while they stood looking down from the summit while munching on a bar of Kendal Mint Cake.

At one time there were many small companies manufacturing mint cake in Kendal, but now there are only three, Romney's, Wilson's and Quiggin's. Romneys were the suppliers to the Everest Expedition, and can also claim to have the original recipe after purchasing Wipers in 1987. Wilsons have been in existence since 1913 and also manufacture speciality chocolates, toffees and fudges. Quiggins is the oldest of the three, being founded in 1840 on the Isle of Man. The factory at Kendal was first established in 1880.

The recipe is very simple. Sugar, glucose and water are mixed together and boiled vigorously whilst being stirred. Peppermint oil is added at a ratio of half an ounce to every 40 pounds of mixture and stirred in. The boiling mixture is then poured in to moulds and allowed to set. There are three main types of mint cake, white made from white sugar, brown from brown sugar and a chocolate-covered mint cake. Hardness and texture vary between manufacturers, and some bars are so sweet that they will set your teeth on edge.

I will still require plenty of energy to finish the walk so I purchase a couple of bars to sustain me through the rest of my journey.

Katherine Parr

To the east of the town stands the ruin of Kendal Castle. The ruin stands on an elongated mound overlooking the town and the River Kent. The castle was built in the 12th century but fell into ruin towards the end of the Tudor Period.

Kendal Castle was the home of the Parr family, and it is alleged that Katherine Parr, the sixth wife of Henry VIII, was born in the castle and spent her early years here. Apart from the fact that she was not one of the wives who met an untimely end at the wrong end of an axe, what else is known about Katherine?

Katherine Parr was born on 11th November 1512. Her father was Sir Thomas Parr, a descendant of Edward III. Her mother was Maud Green, who later became an attendant to Catherine of Aragon.

Most people know that Henry VIII was England's most married King, but very few will point to Katherine Parr as being England's most married Queen. Katherine tied the knot four times and was a major influence on several of the "movers and shakers" of her time.

Husband number one was Edward Borough who Katherine married in 1529 when she was seventeen years old. Little is known of this relationship other than the young Edward did not enjoy the best of health and died in the spring of 1533.

A little of a year later and Katherine was married again. This time it was to a Yorkshireman, John Neville, the 3rd Baron Latymer. The early years of the marriage were a tumultuous time in the north of England. There was much unrest over the separation of the church from Rome, and the dissolution of the monasteries. There was an uprising in York, known to historians as "The Pilgrimage of Grace" and Katherine was taken hostage by the northern rebels. Eventually the uprising was suppressed following assurances and promises by the King and Katherine was released.

John Neville died in 1543, leaving Katherine as a rich widow. Katherine then embarked on a relationship with Sir Thomas Seymour, (brother of Jane Seymour), but somebody else has his beady eye on the merry widow. In those days whatever the King wanted the King got. In this case the King wanted Katherine Parr and the developing relationship with Sir Thomas was ended and Katherine became the sixth wife of Henry VIII on 12th July 1543 at Hampton Court Palace.

In addition to becoming Queen of England on her marriage, Katherine also acquired the title of the first Queen of Ireland after Henry had adopted the title of "King of Ireland" to add to his English crown.

The marriage gave Katherine what today we would term an "instant family". Mary, daughter of Catherine of Aragon was the eldest at 27 years old and only four years younger than Katherine herself. Elizabeth, the daughter of Anne Boleyn, was ten years old. Edward, the son of Jane Seymour was a mere six years of age at the time of the wedding. Owing to the previous behaviour of Henry with respect to their mothers the relationship between the two step-sisters was understandably fractious to say the least. Added to this Henry had removed both Mary and Elizabeth from the line of succession by declaring them both to be illegitimate. Katherine seems to have had a major influence on her step-children and was responsible for establishing some reconciliation between the step-sisters and their father. These reconciliations with his children resulted in Henry allowing Mary and Elizabeth to return to the line of succession for the crown.

Katherine was no wilting wallflower at court, and held the respect and trust not only of Henry himself but many of the courtiers as well. Such was his level of respect for Katherine that

Henry made her his Regent between July and September 1544 when he embarked on his unsuccessful military campaign to France. During her time as Regent, Katherine became known for her strong grasp of the issues of state, showing great character and dignity in the way that she carried out the duties of office. It is believed that this had a great influence on the young Elizabeth who would later try to emulate her step-mother's behaviour when she became Queen herself.

Religion was a hot topic during these times and Katherine had her own independent views on the subject. She was brought up to be a Catholic, but over the years gradually accumulated some strong Protestant tendencies that caused some concern among leading Catholic figures of the day. In particular Katherine had disagreements with the Bishop of Winchester (Stephen Gardiner) and the Lord Chancellor (Lord Wriothesley) who attempted to have the Queen imprisoned for her views. Katherine would also argue with the King about various aspects of religion. Knowing how Henry had been known to act against those who dared to disagree with him this was probably not the wisest move that the Queen could make. Fortunately for Katherine, King Henry was not of the frame of mind to replace her with yet another newer model, and so she was able to continue at the Royal Court and avoid imprisonment or worse.

Henry died on 28th January 1547 at the age of 55 years. There were no definitive reasons given at the time, but modern historians tend towards him suffering from diabetes. In his will

Henry left Katherine an allowance of £7,000 per year, an enormous sum in those days. He also declared that Katherine should still be treated as the Queen for the rest of her life. All this left Katherine a very wealthy and high status lady, and still only 34 years old.

What do you think that Katherine did next? Yes, that's correct. She went straight back to Lord Thomas Seymour, who by this time had taken the title of Lord Seymour of Sudeley. They married quickly and Katherine became pregnant for the first time. Katherine gave birth to a daughter, Mary Seymour, on 30th August 1548. Joy at the birth was short-lived. Hygiene in Tudor times was almost non-existent and Katherine fell victim to puerperal fever, also known as "childbed fever". It was a fairly common cause of death to mothers and was generally caused by lack of hygiene at the birth. Katherine died six days later on 5th September 1548 aged only 35 years. Her remains are buried in a marble tomb at St.Mary's Chapel at Sudeley Castle, near to Winchcombe in Gloucestershire.

Thomas Seymour did not survive much longer. He had been involved in some shady dealings with various rebel groups and was found guilty of treason and executed only a few months later. Mary was taken into care by the Dowager Duchess of Suffolk who had been a friend of Katherine. There are no records of Mary after her second birthday and it is believed that she died when still a young child.

Alfred Wainwright

There are names that will be forever associated with specific activities. Football has Mathews and Finney, rowing will always have Redgrave and boxing will always remember Muhammad Ali. Walking is no exception and the name instantly recognised by all is that of Alfred Wainwright who made his home in Kendal.

Alfred Wainwright was born on January 17th 1907 in Blackburn. His father was a stonemason and the family would have been considered rather poor in today's terms. The young Wainwright left school aged 13 and found a job as an office boy in the Blackburn Corporation Engineers Office. That would appear to have been young Alfred's lot in life, to be spent in hum-drum obscurity. However, in 1930 when he was only 23 years old his life changed unexpectedly.

Wainwright had saved some money from his meagre wages and took a week's holiday in the Lake District with his friend Eric Beardsall. They arrived in Windermere and decided to walk up Orrest Head, a small fell overlooking Windermere. It was a walk that changed Wainwright's life beyond measure. We can only imaging the emotions that swept through his young mind when he looked down on Windermere, and then stared in wonder at the sights of the larger hills in the distance, Scafell Pike, Langdale Pikes and The Old Man of Coniston. Wainwright's love affair with the fells of the Lake District had begun. (Orrest Head is easily accessible from Windermere Station and the views are as magnificent today as they were in Wainwright's time).

In 1931 Wainwright married Ruth Holden and their marriage produced a son, Peter. Alfred continued to visit the fells regularly. In 1940 he achieved another breakthrough by successfully applying for a position in the Borough Treasurer's Office at Kendal. (Wainright's former office in the Council Buildings now houses the town Tourist Information office). His relocation to Kendal enabled him to spend more time in his beloved fells and he started to compile his guidebooks to the area.

Wainwright was excellent at drawing and his skills enabled him to illustrate the guides with pencil sketches. He doggedly wrote the books at the rate of a page every day until he had completed his seven famous volumes "Pictorial Guides to the Lakeland Fells". The books were originally published between 1955 and 1966, but such are their popularity today that you can hardly walk in to any bookshop in Cumbria without finding them on display.

It is a mark of the esteem with which Wainwright is held that his name has become the collective noun for fells among those walkers who like to chase targets by "peak bagging". All of the fells mentioned in the seven books are given the collective name of "Wainwright's". There are 214 of them in total, and a record is kept by the Long Distance Walkers Association of all those names who have successfully completed the ascents of all of them.

Wainwright also compiled the "Pennine Way Companion" in 1968, and in 1972 devised the "Coast to Coast Walk". This starts on the east coast at St Bees head near Workington and crosses the north of England and the Pennines to finish at the Post Office in

Robin Hoods Bay on the west coast. The distance covered is 192 miles and will take the average walker over two weeks to complete.

Alfred Wainwright died of a heart attack on January 20th 1991. In accordance with his last wishes his ashes were scattered at Innominate Tarn near the summit of Haystacks in the northern fells of the Lake District. He is commemorated on a stone tablet set into the windowsill of St James Church, Buttermere. The window fittingly looks out over the slopes of Haystacks.

Chocolate House

If you take the lady in your life to Kendal it is a sure-fire bet that you will end up in the Chocolate House. This establishment in Branthwaite Brow is an attractive stone building overlooking the cobbled street and as its name suggests is dedicated to all things chocolate. To be perfectly accurate it is named Chocolate House 1657 to distinguish itself from all of the younger pretenders.

The original house is thought to have been built around 1630 and was used as a private home. Later it became a bakery and the outline of the ovens can still be seen in the restaurant today. To keep with the theme of former elegance ladies staffing the shop all wear 17th century costume which adds to the atmosphere of the place.

Inside the shop there is wall-to-wall chocolate in exquisite packages. There are chocolates for every occasion, birthdays, weddings or simply just for the pure pleasure of eating chocolate. It is the sort of place where my good lady suddenly develops a huge smile and a spring in her step while I instinctively place a stronger grip on my wallet.

The restaurant serves eighteen different chocolate drinks and on the day I visited had fourteen different types of chocolate gateaux to choose from. When faced with such temptation there is only one thing to do. Give in.

K Shoes

K Shoes had a modest beginning. In 1841 Robert Miller Somervell set up a leather and shoemakers supplies business at the age of twenty-one. In those days every village had its own shoemaker and there were many in the towns. Robert travelled widely and built up a considerable business with the shoemakers of northern England. Within a few years the business had grown to such an extent that it required someone to manage the warehouse while Robert was away drumming up the orders.

In 1848 Robert went into partnership with his younger brother John and the business grew further. Soon they were the second-largest employers in Kendal and started to turn their attention to shoe manufacturing as well as the supplies business. New machinery was introduced and the business continued to expand.

It was in 1865 that an incident occurred that gave K shoes its identity. Whilst all of the boot and shoe uppers were stitched together at the factory it was the usual custom for the soles to be stitched on by outworkers. Some of the more unscrupulous outworkers were substituting lower grade leather soles and using these for their work, at the same time selling on the superior quality soles provided by the factory. For the outworkers this was considered to be a "nice little earner" but understandably the factory supervisors had a different viewpoint. One of them had the bright idea of stamping the leather soles that were provided for outworkers, so identifying the finished shoes and preventing the soles from being sold on. The stamp chosen for this was a letter "K", and so it remained until the factory finally closed. Why it was a "K" is a mystery, it was probably just one of those things that happens. It would have been more logical to have chosen an "S" for Somervell but there we are. The key thing is that this simple security measure worked and the "K" mark became synonymous with shoe quality. When the first Trade Mark Acts came into force in 1875 the Somervells had to fight to keep the mark because single letter trademarks were banned under the terms of the acts. However, because the "K" had been acknowledged for more than ten years they were allowed to be an exception. Up until the present day there has not been any other single letter trademark that has been recognised by the UK trademark administrations.

The enterprise continued to grow as the next generation of Somervells took over the reigns. At the end of the 19th century the factory was producing almost 200,000 pairs of footwear a year. By 1920 the demand for K Shoes was such that there was not enough capacity in the workforce to operate solely from Kendal and an extra factory was opened at Lancaster.

During the Second World War the factory concentrated on Government contract work, not only for Servicemen's boots and shoes but also kitbags, tents, gaiters and all sorts of items for use by the forces. There was a special "Airman's Flying Boot" that contained secret compartments for stowing away materials that could later be used for escaping from capture if they were shot down by the enemy.

After hostilities ended the company continued to prosper with ever-increasing demand. More new factories were opened in the north, including Workington, Millom and Shap, and even one in Norwich. At its peak there were nine factories producing 130,000 pairs of "K" footwear every week.

Footwear manufacturing is a labour intensive industry and was very susceptible to attack from cheap imports. The decline in demand started to show through in the mid 1970's but once it had started swept rapidly like a forest fire through the entire British footwear industry. Workers were laid off and costs were cut but the rise of the cheap imports was relentless. Factories were closed and in a desperate attempt to keep what was left remaining of the British shoe industry the two great competitors, "K" Shoes and C & J Clarke merged together. Even this was not enough and a steady stream of redundancies continued. The last pair of shoes to be made at Kendal were stitched on May 2nd 2003 and the factory closed. An industry that had once given employment to 20% of the people of Kendal was no more.

DAY SIX

BURNESIDE TO BOWNESS

9.8 MILES

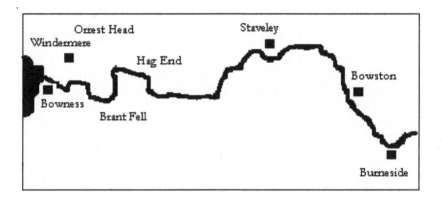

<u>Westmorland</u>

Westmorland is one of the old 39 counties of England. As always seems to be the case, the first written records start with the Domesday Book of 1086. Here I find that the area in those days was mainly divided up between Yorkshire and Cumberland. Some parts were even considered to be in Scotland and were a part of the ancient Kingdom of Strathclyde.

In 1092 King William II created the twin Baronies of Kendal and Westmorland, which were later merged into the single county of Westmorland in 1226. The ancient boundaries were formed by Lancashire to the south, Cumbria to the north, and Yorkshire and County Durham to the East. My journey will take me to the very edge of the old county, for Lake Windermere formed part of the western border. The boundary also just creeps around the outer fringe of Helvellyn, making it the highest point in Westmorland at 3117ft (950m). The former county town was Appleby, most known for its annual horse fair.

Westmorland was a victim of the Boundary Commission in 1974 when it was incorporated into the new county of Cumbria by combining it with Cumberland. It was really no surprise, for the 1971 census showed that Westmorland, with a population of only 70,000 was the second least populated county after Rutland, which also disappeared in the same re-organisation.

The area is distinctly different from the harsher surroundings of the Lake District. It has more gentle slopes and undulations than its neighbour, with a more open feeling to it. Many people pass the area by in their haste to reach the Lake District. If you are one try taking a later turn off the M6 and enjoy the delights of the lovely Kent Valley.

Postman Pat

For one man the area had a simplistic beauty that he transferred to books and the small screen to the delight of children. Here in Westmorland John Arthur Cunliffe found the inspiration for Greendale, where Pat Clifton and his cat Jess delivered the daily post to the local residents.

John Cunliffe based Greendale on Longsleddale which is just north of Kendal. It is not on the Dales Way, but some things just have to be done and a motorised diversion is called for to enable me to sample the delights of Longsleddale.

The turning off the A6 is small and we nearly miss it. A small solitary finger-board bearing the name "Longsleddale" is all that marks the gateway to the valley. I am half-expecting to see large boards proclaiming "Welcome to Greendale – Home of Postman Pat", or "Postman Pat World – Coaches Welcome". Fortunately the commercial world is yet to force these monstrosities on this picturesque part of the Dales and long may it continue to be so.

The narrow road follows the River Sprint up Longsleddale and the first delight is discovering that the road is lined on both sides by drystone walls just like I have seen on the television! Surely there is not a hump-backed bridge as well? Yes there is! Oh wonderful!

Unfortunately there is no Post Office in Longsleddale. The inspiration for that is back at Kendal where John Cunliffe imagined Mrs. Goggins sitting behind the counter at the Beast Banks Post

Office. The office unfortunately closed in 2003 and is now simply known as 10, Greenside but it has not been forgotten. Kendal Civic Society has put a red plaque on the wall of the house to commemorate the connection between Kendal and Postman Pat.

Postman Pat was first screened in 1981 and was an instant hit with young children. The simple tales of Postman Pat always lending a helping hand to the people of Greendale as he made his delivery rounds enchanted parent and child alike.

So popular and well-known did Postman Pat become that Royal Mail adopted the character as a marketing tool, but later dropped their support in 2001 claiming that Pat no longer fitted with their "corporate image". Presumably this was because Pat's reputation for ever-reliable delivery was something beyond the comprehension of the Royal Mail management! Pat in turn no longer gives free publicity to that body, but now works for an organisation known as "Special Delivery Service". That must be one in the eye for the suits at the Royal Mail.

Pat was fortunate to always have a private number plate on his vehicle. PAT1 was based on the standard red Royal Mail Bedford HA van. When post buses became all the rage in rural areas Pat traded up to one of those, having the number plate PAT2. From series 4 the bus was painted yellow so that it could double up as the school bus.

Once free of the restrictions of Royal Mail Pat could literally fly. Special Delivery Service gave him the use of a helicopter PAT3.

He also had a brand new mini van PAT4 and a shiny new motorcycle which inevitable displayed PAT5.

It is childish, but as we drive along the road we cannot help but burst into song;

Postman Pat, Postman Pat,
Postman Pat with his black and white cat,
Early in the morning,
Just as day is dawning,
He picks up all the postbags in his van.

Postman Pat, Postman Pat,
Postman Pat with his black and white cat,
All the birds are singing,
As the day is just beginning,
Pat feels he's a really happy man.

The road undulates along the valley floor, passing a succession of houses dotted along the road. Altogether there are about thirty houses and approximately eighty people who live in the valley, plus an estimated 5,000 sheep. The sheep are easily seen but the other residents of the Longsleddale are much more difficult to find. I am assured that deer, badgers and red squirrels are often seen in the valley but today they are making themselves scarce. In the air buzzards, kestrels and owls can often be sighted while they seek out their prey. Along the riverbank herons and kingfishers wait to dart into the waters to obtain their fish supper.

It is indeed a beautifully scenic dale and well worth the diversion I have made. There are small car parks opposite St.Mary's Church and at the top of the road that enable walkers to leave their vehicles and explore the fell-side. Much of the hillside is protected as a "Site of Special Scientific Interest" due to the wide range of flora and fauna that can be found here. It is all very verdant. The hedgerows are a bright green and I can see bluebells forming patches of carpet under the woodland canopy.

It would have been just too much for a red post-van to appear, although there are regular deliveries made along the dale. To the best of my knowledge the postman carries out his round on his own, without the assistance of a black-and-white cat.

Burneside

On the face of it most people assume that the name for Burneside is obvious. When one pauses and remembers that burn is in fact a Scottish word, and that there are no "burns" in the Lake District then a more obscure derivation is required. In this case the name, (as has so often been the case on this walk) has Norse origins. It comes from Bronolf's Head and in its early days was known as Burneshead.

Prosperity came to Burneside with the paper mill. This was purchased by James Cropper in 1845.

Records show that a corn mill has existed at Burneside since the early 13th century. Over the years this was adapted into a wool mill and a cotton mill, but in the early 1800's it was converted to a paper mill. When the lease was purchased in 1845 by James Cropper the mill gained a new lease of life and business boomed.

The mill is still very much a going concern over 150 years later, manufacturing all types of specialist papers. How the business has grown can be measured by the transport systems used. During the early days raw materials and finished goods were transported by two pack horses, in 1879 a tramline was installed to link the mill to Kendal. This was improved to a railway line in 1927, and now a whole fleet of lorries is used to distribute the goods.

Burneside is my starting point for the last day. The weather is ideal. The sun is shining, there is a gentle cooling breeze and it is shirt-sleeve time. It is all so different to a couple of days ago.

The walk from Burneside to Staveley is a delight. The route follows the River Kent all of the way and the birds and insects are zooming about their daily business.

The River Kent is reputed to be one of the fastest flowing rivers in England. I do not know how these things are measured, but carrying all of the extra water from several days of rainfall it is certainly racing along this morning.

Staveley

The penultimate settlement on the walk, Staveley has been in existence here in some form since around 4000BC. Celtic-Britons farmed the area for four millennia until the Romans arrived to shatter their peace.

Staveley is derived from the Old English, Staeff Leah, meaning Staff Pasture.

With a plentiful supply of water from the rivers Kent and Gowan to drive machinery the locality has for centuries been very much an industrial village. The largest industry at one time was bobbin-turning and this reached a peak during the 1850's. The industry entered a sharp decline following the introduction of child-labour restrictions in 1863, and by 1871 almost all of the bobbin work had ceased.

For the connoisseur of English heritage buildings a visit to the church of St James is a must. The church was built in 1684 – 1685 and houses some exquisite stained-glass windows designed by Edward Burne-Jones and manufactured by the William Morris Company.

The Dales Way only just kisses the southern edge of Staveley before darting off through a gap between the houses to resume open countryside again.

To the north of the town is the beautiful Kentmere valley which can only be accessed through Staveley. It is well worth a visit and there is a bus that travels up and down the valley during the summer months for the benefit of visitors who can get on or off as they please.

Leaving Staveley behind there are only six miles until I reach my final destination. It is a pleasant stroll along undulating pastures and isolated hedge-lined country lanes, all the time admiring the views of the Westmorland countryside.

An entertaining interlude was a section known as "Little Lakeland", undulating land dotted with small rocky outcrops and bright yellow gorse bushes. The path swerves its way between the gorse, twisting this way and all the while bobbing up and down like a small roller-coaster.

Not long after this I pass by a fascinating water feature near Crag House Farm. A spring spurts its water out into a small pool. And that is it. The whole thing can not be more than ten feet square. So what you may say? You can see those in garden centres up and down the country. Yes indeed, but they have electric pumps in them to circulate the water. What we have here is a water feature developed by nature that forces water to the surface, pours it into a pool where the water level appears to stay constant. So how does it do that? Where does the water come from? Where does it go?

I am conscious that the path is taking me slowly and steadily downhill and the distant hills of the Lake District are gradually coming to dominate the skyline. I pass by the farm at Hag End and just when it looks as though I am going to have one more hill to climb the Dales Way takes a sharp left turn to join a track that heads due south and continues with the descent.

The ground levels off and I pass by the edge of Matson Grounds Farm. This is a fully certified "organic" farm specializing in prime lamb and beef.

I am passing through more woodland than I have encountered for a good while. Most of the last two days have been spent walking in very open countryside. The hills of the Lake District are close now. The Coniston Fells and Langdale Pikes are clearly in view, and as I steadily draw nearer to the distant rooftops of Bowness there are the occasional glimpses of the waters of Windermere through the trees.

The path contours around Brant Fell and the final descending slopes stretch ahead, dropping towards Bowness and the shimmering lake beyond. This must be one of the most beautiful last stretches of the long distance footpaths in England. To the north there is the small fell of Orrest Head, where Alfred Wainwright was so struck by the beauty before him that he devoted his life to exploring the hills of the Lake District. The clouds of previous days have departed leaving the sun to illuminate the mountain tops with its rays, and speckles of light glisten off the waters of Windermere below. It is a place to rest a while and allow the beauty of nature to absorb into the memory.

There is a final marker, a slate seat almost identical to the one that I started from at Ilkley. The plaque by the seat also reads "For those who walk the Dales Way". The stone seat signifies that my journey is nearly done. Not quite finished though, because I have a few streets of Bowness to explore before I reach my absolute destination, the shoreline of Windermere.

Bowness-on-Windermere

It is often a shock to many people when they first realise that the major town for Windermere is actually Bowness and not the small town one and a half miles away from the water. For this they can blame the coming of the railway in 1847. When the link was put in from the west-coast mainline at Oxenholme to Bowness it was terminated at the small village of Birthwaite. In order to boost passenger traffic and make it clear where the ultimate destination was intended to be the marketing men named the terminus "Windermere". Within a relatively short time the village also became known as Windermere and changed its name accordingly. Windermere and Bowness gradually became considered to be one town, and in 1974 were formed into a single civil parish.

Bowness boomed, and wealthy Lancashire businessmen built elegant houses overlooking the waters. Most of the houses have since been converted to hotels and guest-houses to accommodate the still-growing numbers of visitors who flock to the area. The town is a tourist honeypot with bustling activity both in the town centre and along the esplanade. There are literally thousands of boats moored in the marinas and there is a continuous "clink-clink" of sail fittings chinking against the metal masts of the yachts.

Lakeland Plastics

There are many (including my dearly beloved) for whom no visit to the Lake District would ever be fully complete without searching through the shelves at Lakeland. The store is the flag-ship of the Lakeland kitchen-gadget empire and it contains an amazing collection of gizmos.

The business was founded in 1956 by Alan Rayner. He was an agricultural feed salesman and one day had the bright idea of selling polythene bags to his customers to pack poultry in for market. The business expanded and together with his wife Dorothy Rayner found himself running a successful business providing agricultural plastics and food freezing plastics. With the booming popularity in the use of domestic home freezers there was an enthusiastic market for the products via mail-order and the business started to soar. It was but a small step from that point to supplying other kitchen utensils and the venture went into overdrive. Lakeland currently has 42 stores around the country and a massive mail-order catalogue and web-ordering service. A range of over 4,000 products fulfils every kitchen and garden need that you could possibly think of. The company is still a family business currently run by the Managing Director Sam Rayner.

Beatrix Potter

Bowness also has some literary history. Further up the valley in Grassmere Wordsworth wandered "lonely as a cloud" but alongside the shores of Windermere things were a lot livelier and aimed at the younger generations. Arthur Ransome set his series of children's adventure stories "Swallows and Amazons" in locations at Windermere and Coniston. Those familiar with his works will be able to identify the town of Bowness as Ransome's fictional town of Rio. Beatrix Potter made her home at Sawrey on the opposite bank of Windermere to Bowness. The visitor can hardly move around Bowness without continually being faced with images of Peter Rabbit and his friends. There is an excellent exhibition of "The World of Beatrix Potter" where you can see children wide-eyed with delight as they meet Mrs. Tiggy-Winkle in her kitchen or see Mr. McGregor' in his garden.

Beatrix Potter was born in South Kensington, London, on July 28th 1866. Her parents were relatively well-to-do from inherited income but were not exactly dynamic. Father Rupert was a barrister but spent most of his time in the London Gentlemen's Clubs, and mother Helen spent her days in social visiting. Young Beatrix was kept mostly in the house with her governess. Beatrix kept a large number of pets including two rabbits, Peter and Benjamin, who would soon become immortalised in her works. She would spend hours watching her pets and drawing them, and soon became very skilful at representing their different moods with pencil and paper.

Rupert Potter would rent a house for the summer, usually in Scotland, but one year when Beatrix was sixteen he rented Wray Castle on the shores of Windermere. The family became friendly with the vicar of Wray Church, Canon Hardwicke Rownsley. Rownsley was concerned about the potential environmental damage of industrial activity to the tranquility of the Lake District and Beatrix was greatly influenced by his love for the countryside. (Rownsley was such an enthusiastic campaigner for the environment that he would later become one of the founders of the National Trust).

The family continued to visit on an annual basis, and one year when she returned to London Beatrix started to make greetings cards from the sketches she had drawn. At the same time she started a book about the adventures of a young rabbit.

"The Tale of Peter Rabbit" was published in 1902 and the lonely life of Miss Potter was to change for ever. The book generated income that finally gave her some independence from her parents. Her next books "The Tale of Squirrel Nutkin", "Tale of the Tailor of Gloucester" and "Tale of Benjamin Bunny" generated enough income to enable Beatrix to purchase Hill Top Farm near Sawrey. This was the start of her "farm empire" and she continued to buy farms in the area. In 1930 Potter purchased the Monk Coniston Estate which included the area known as Tarn Hows, one of the most photographed scenes in the Lake District.

Beatrix married local solicitor William Heelis in 1913. When she passed away on December 22nd 1943 Beatrix Potter bequeathed 14 farms and 40,000 acres of land to the National Trust, preserving the beauty of the Lake District for generations to come as her legacy. Hardwicke Rownsley would have been proud of her.

Windermere

How many lakes are there in the Lake District? It is one of those trick questions beloved of the saloon-bar clever-dick. The grammatically correct answer is that there is only one. Bassenthwaite Lake is the only waterway in the area that contains the word "lake" in its official name. All of the others already have the Old English word "Mere" in their name. The correct nomenclature for the largest piece of inland water in England is simply Windermere and not as is commonly believed Lake Windermere.

Windermere derives its name from Old Norse, originally being known as Vinandr's Mere. The water runs almost directly on a north-south line and is 10.5 miles long. It measures 1 mile at its broadest point and is up to 220 feet deep. The greatest depths are to be found towards the north end of the lake. There are 18 islands, the largest of which is the privately owned Belle Island near Bowness which has an area of 16 hectares.

The Freshwater Biological Association was set up in 1929 to study the ecology of the lake, and has its headquarters at Far Sawrey, directly opposite to Bowness. Trout, charr, pike and perch are the largest fish that inhabit the lake, although in common with most other large areas of water there are stories of "monsters of the deep". In the case of Windermere this is alleged to be a giant eel-like creature, although as often seems to be the case the only people who claim to have seen it usually only do so at night, and then only after spending some considerable time in a local hostelry.

According to one source I found there are over 10,000 boats registered for use on the water. This looks easily the case when the visitor views rows upon rows of white-hulled vessels lined up on the moorings at Bowness and Waterhead. What would happen if they were all on the water at the same time defies thinking about. Somebody must have thought about it though, because in March 2005 a speed limit was imposed on Windermere for the first time.

`The speed limit was imposed much too late to stop various water-speed record attempts many years ago. Sir Henry Seagrove perished after capsizing his boat "Miss England II" on Friday 13th June 1930 after achieving a new world record of 98.76mph. Water speed events later moved to nearby Coniston Water. Although Coniston is significantly shorter it has the advantage that not only were there significantly less boats on it, but also that it has no island obstructions. Without having to dodge around the islands that are dotted across Windermere, in particular the large Belle Isle just off Bowness, the speedboats could travel much further in a straight line on Coniston Water and therefore attain higher speeds.

I may have got very wet during the last few days, and also experienced some very chilling winds. Despite all the moaning I can generally cope with all the discomfort that entails and in a short time can enthusiastically set off again on another venture. However there is nothing that would induce me to participate in the latest recreational challenge on (or more accurately in) Windermere. Last year over two thousand people willingly plunged into the blood-chilling waters to take part in the first "Great North Swim". Later this year over 6,000 will take part, and who knows how many will venture forth in future knowing the way these things tend to escalate. The first winner in 2008 was Welshman David Davies who was a medal winner at the Beijing Olympic Games. The race is held in September and more information can be found at www.greatswim.org

The west shore is almost entirely owned by the National Trust and there is an excellent walk along the shoreline. The walk is best reached by taking the ferry across from Bowness to Castle Wray and then walking down the side of the lake and catching a return Ferry either from Sawrey or for the more ambitious walker from the southern end of the lake at Lakeside.

Journey's End

The gleaming white walls of "The Royal Oak" greet me at the bottom of Brantfell Road. A large sign mounted on the wall draws me like a magnet. "Rest your weary legs, enjoy our fine ales and indulge in our home cooked food" declared the inviting message. The "dearly beloved" will be waiting for me at the lakeside so after a brief hesitation I decide to plod on. Then I realise that there are more words on the sign. "Official Finishing Pub for the

Dales Way" it shouts at me. Well, if it's official I can hardly just ignore it can I?

Having refreshingly fulfilled my official obligations I take the last steps of my journey to the esplanade and the only thing in front of me now is the ferry jetty. Well, that and all of the people.

The esplanade in front of the landing staging is a very popular place for visitors to congregate and I would imagine that most tourists end up here at some point. There are all ages here, young and old and empty seats are always quickly snapped up. Many of the children become absorbed by feeding the multitude of swans and ducks that also congregate here. Child and bird enjoy a synergy here; the child is here because this is where the swans and ducks are, while at the same time the waterfowl are here because this is where the humans come with bags of delicious bread crumbs!

My final objective is a low building laying a short distance to my left; the Tourist Information Centre. Fixed against the outside wall is an information board with a large map showing the route of the Dales Way from the start in Ilkley to the Windermere shore at Bowness. I have stood here and looked at the map before, but then it was merely a map marked with places. This time it was different. The names and places were vividly transformed in my mind into all of the wonderful memories of the last six days.

ACKNOWLEDGEMENTS

To Norina, described herein as "dearly beloved", for all of the transport to and from the various start and finish points.

To all of the many people I met during my journey that provided information for the book.

REFERENCES

Information was gathered from many sources including guidebooks, notice boards, information leaflets and the internet. The following is not an exclusive list, but do contain more information for the reader to discover.

General Information

Dales Way	www.dalesway.org.uk
Yorkshire Dales National Park	www.yorkshiredales.org.uk
Yorkshire Dales	www.yorkshire-dales.com
Cumbria	www.visitcumbria.com
National Trust	www.nationaltrust.org.uk
Lake District	www.english-lakes.com
Wikipedia	www.wikipedia.org

Long Distance Walks

The Walking Englishman	www.walkingenglishman.co.uk

Specific Websites

Ilkley	www.ilkley.org.uk
Bettys Tea Rooms	www.bettys.co.uk
Ilkley Toy Museum	www.ilkleytoymuseum.co.uk
Addingham	www.addinghamonline.co.uk
River Wharfe Fly Fishing	www.yorkshire-dales-flyfishing.com
Bolton Abbey	www.boltonabbey.com
Embsay & Bolton Railway	www.embsayboltonrailway.org.uk

The Bodger	www.flyingshavings.co.uk
Burnsall Sports	www.burnsallsports.co.uk
Grassington	www.grassington.co.uk
Kettlewell	www.kettlewell.info.uk
Buckden	www.buckden.org.uk
UK Agriculture	www.ukagriculture.com
National Sheep Association	www.nationalsheep.org.uk
J.B.Priestley	www.jbpriestleysociety.com
Drystone Walling	www.dswa.org.uk
Limestone Pavements	www.limestone-pavements.org
Settle to Carlisle Railway	www.settle-carlisle.co.uk
Dent Heritage Centre	www. dentvillageheritagecentre.com
Dent Brewery	www.dentbrewery.co.uk
Sedbergh School	www.sedberghschool.org.uk
Sedbergh	www.sedbergh.org
Briggflatts	www. briggflatts.org
Quaker Tapestry	www.quaker-tapestry.co.uk
Snuff	www. samuelgawith.co.uk
Chocolate House	www.chocolatehouse1657.co.uk
Alfred Wainwright	www.wainwright.org
Kendal Mint Cake	www.kendalmintcake.co.uk
James Cropper	www.jamescropper.com
Longsleddale	www.longsleddale.co.uk
Lakeland	www.lakeland.co.uk
Freshwater Biological Ass.	www.fba.org